Mind the Gap

True stories of
year-out projects

Edited by Cathie Bartlam

Scripture Union

© Scripture Union 1999
First published 1999

Scripture Union, 207–209 Queensway, Bletchley, Milton Keynes,
MK2 2EB

ISBN 1 85999 324 9

British Library Cataloguing-in-Publication Data.
A catalogue record of this book is available from the British library.

Printed and bound in Great Britain by
Cox and Wyman Ltd, Reading, Berkshire

Contents

The gap

It is becoming increasingly possible for young people to have a 'gap' when they finish school and before they go to University or start college. What can you do with this gap, whether it is a few weeks, months or a full year? Some people study another subject, some work and save up money, others go travelling and still others decide to do something different with their time.

This book tells the true stories of young people whose gap weeks, or months, were used in doing things they had never done before or visiting places they had only read about. Their situations are all different but the common thread that links these stories together is that all the young people are Christians. All would say that whatever they did they learned a lot about themselves, about other people and about God.

Prepare to be amazed, amused, excited and challenged by these frank stories.

They may give you ideas for planning a gap project of your own. There is a list of opportunities and organisations at the end of the book.

Monkey business and the peanut seller

Name:	Jo Taylor
Organisation:	Scripture Union
Destination:	Southern India
Mission:	practical work, helping with Holiday Bible Schools

The monkey troupe sauntered one by one across the kids' playground. I was the first to spot them and ran out of the staff-room to get a closer look. A male monkey about half my size stared at me as I waved my hands and shouted at it to leave the playground. It was at times like these that I wondered what I was doing in India organising a Bible camp for two hundred kids. The monkeys made their way into the classrooms and started to help themselves to the kids' lunches. We were hoping to have a shared lunch later that day. It looked as if there was not going to be any food to share unless we got rid of the monkeys.

There are a few problems with being female in India. Firstly, if you are white you get stared at a lot, especially on buses and, secondly, the monkeys take no notice of women. My manic shouts finally led to my fellow Indian co-workers, who were totally used to monkeys, rousing themselves from their coffee break to come to my aid. The only man, Anand, approached the monkeys cautiously with a bit of hand waving. After much coaxing from the rest of us he started to shout loudly. The leading male monkey got the message and they scampered back up the trees. The timing was perfect as the bell rang for morning break and the kids poured out of assembly. Another minor crisis was over. Only a few lunches had gone missing, tears were soon dried with promises to share all the rest of the food and I said I would supply some chocolate.

I was in Vellore taking part in a ten-day Vacation Bible School (VBS). It was mid-April and I had been in India for ten weeks and generally loved every second of it. I had arrived at the beginning of February with two English guys, Paul and Joe, and this was the first time in Vellore that I was by myself with an all-Indian team. Paul was on another team somewhere else in the city and Joe was at another VBS in the inner city of Chennai (formerly Madras).

Vellore is famous for its hospital and we were actually living on the hospital campus. We stayed in a beautiful empty house usually used by a doctor. We could have breakfast and lunch at the canteen. The food took some getting used to! Every night we were invited round to different doctors' houses for dinner.

The team was excellent and we all became good friends. I particularly enjoyed being with Pauline. I had met her at Cornerstone House in Mahabalipuram. This was my home base while in India and is run by Rod and Ruthie Gilbert. They are the most amazing couple. They looked after me like a daughter while I stayed with them. Pauline had been attending a marriage course run at Cornerstone House. That had opened my eyes to a totally different way of doing things. It took me a while to understand and appreciate the whole idea of arranged marriage. Pauline and I became good friends and by the time we were in Vellore I had already been up to her home in Chennai for a visit.

When I knew that I would be spending time with an all-Indian team away from Cornerstone House I was quite daunted. However it was amazing to experience how much God was in it. The rest of the team, Pauline, Amand, Chittra and Susan, our leader, were ace. I loved being with them. It was brilliant to witness the many older kids who renewed their commitment to God at the end of the ten-day camp. I learned a lot about South Indian culture and how different it is to my own Western one. My team were all over twenty years old but the respect they had for their elders was incredible. It is not like that in England. By eighteen you are supposed to be an adult and independent. In India you are never truly independent of your family. They play a massive part in their young people's lives, especially in major decisions like education and marriage.

I had chosen to take a year out after my GCSEs due to illness but by October '96 I was better and bored. I read about Cornerstone House and Scripture Union's work in Mahabalipuram in SU's *Outreach* magazine. The article gave a contact number for anyone interested in short-term volunteer work. By Christmas it was all arranged.

Nothing can prepare you for India: the noise, the smells, the crowds of people. You never see an empty street and everywhere you look there are cows, the Hindus' sacred animals.

I spent two weeks touring the north of the country with Paul, Joe and a New Zealander, Carolyn. We saw the Taj Mahal in Agra, had our noses pierced (painful) and finally made it to Delhi. India's capital is massive and there are millions of people wherever you go. We stayed in a tourist area near the main station. Hotel rooms are ridiculously cheap compared to the West and we paid under £5 a night for a room. Delhi was how I had imagined it. Tiny little streets led to crowded bazaars, filled with chattering people, autos and cows. Autos, also known as rickshaws, are the best way to get around the crowded cities. They are like three-wheeled motorbikes with a back seat on which you can squash four people. I had never seen anything like this mad city which never seemed to sleep.

The contrast between the rich and poor was so intense it was almost blinding. After a while you just seem to get used to seeing the skinny beggar on the street, ignored by the beautiful rich Indian women dripping with gold jewellery.

One night we were all trying to find a place to eat and were wandering through the usual crowds when we saw a peanut seller shouting and beating a tiny street child. Carolyn, who had gone to school in India when she was young, was appalled at the sight so she grabbed my hand and pulled me over to the peanut seller. She shouted at him while I grabbed the child. He could not have been more than five years old. He had matted hair and was wearing only shorts. His older sister appeared out of the crowd. She was equally skinny, looked about twelve years old and was carrying a toddler. She also began shouting at the peanut seller in broken English, 'Hitting, hitting, bad man hitting!' In India if someone does something wrong in a public place the best thing is to be really loud about it and make a fuss. This then shames the culprit, who becomes very apologetic. The peanut seller was extremely embarrassed even though he tried to explain that the boy had been stealing peanuts. This was still not a good enough excuse to beat a child. By now quite a crowd had gathered so the seller shoved a bag of peanuts into the boy's hand and moved off. I put the little boy down and Carolyn and I looked at each other. We were both thinking the same thing. We could not just leave these three kids here but what other choice did we have? In broken Hindi Carolyn asked where their parents were but the older girl just shrugged her shoulders and looked at the floor. My heart felt like breaking but there was nothing we could do except buy them some food and give them a few rupees. Then they disappeared into the crowd.

You see street kids wherever you go in India. Poverty is a reality of everyday life for thousands of kids. Once in Chennai Central Train Station a few kids came up to me asking for money. It is really hard to say no. When you are white they think you have lots of money, which you do in comparison to them. So I always gave the kids what change I had. On this occasion I bought about eight packets of biscuits and sat on the platform with about fifteen kids and shared them out. This was a crazy thing to do as kids appear from everywhere and they are not exactly into sharing. You should have seen the looks I got from the Indian passengers who were waiting for their trains. They thought I was totally mad. One of my Christian Indian friends was with me.

'I've never thought of buying the kids food,' he said. 'I hardly ever give money as it encourages them to beg more, but food, that's a good idea.'

In India I was encouraged by something Jackie Pullinger said about it being better to give than have a hard heart.

I found a lot of my western views challenged in India. I was driving to Chengleputt with Luke Gilbert who was born in India and has lived there all his life. I saw a crippled dog by the side of the road and commented about the general mistreatment of animals in India. His response stunned me. He said that he would bet that I had more compassion for the dog than I did for a disabled person by the side of the road.

I realised that there were many times in England and India when I had walked past a homeless person on the street or ignored the disabled person begging. If I saw an injured animal, though, I was totally there for it and tried to help. It is not that helping sick animals is wrong but it is a matter of priorities and mine were typically western. I found that God really sorted out my views on certain issues and when I came home I was much more willing to help the homeless person as well as the injured animal.

I also began to take more seriously issues like education. I realised how privileged I was to have access to an education and to some of the best universities in the world. I vowed that when I returned home I would not abuse the privileges God has given me by just being born in England, but I would use them to glorify him.

As I write this, it has been over a year since I returned to England. My gap year was one of the best things I have ever done. I am now halfway through my A levels and am looking forward to another gap year before university, working for my church as a youth worker.

I miss India every day and I do not know what the future holds. If I get the chance and God wants me to, I will be back in India as soon as possible.

Travels with a truck

Name:	Joe Bean
Organisation:	Scripture Union
Destination:	Southern India
Mission:	practical work; building

It was ten in the evening on a starry night in South India. All was quiet and peaceful but Paul and I were getting fidgety because the truck we were waiting for was now ten hours late. For it to have arrived on time would have been unheard of. Two hours late would be reasonable, but ten? Even on Indian time that was a bit much.

The truck had been hired to transport Paul, me and a huge heap of building equipment from the Scripture Union centre on the beach at Mahabalipuram to the newly bought camp site at Avalanche Lake some two hundred kilometres away. This was over two thousand metres up in the Nilgiri Hills. During May a work camp was to take place when volunteers from all over India would converge on this remote spot in the wilds for a month of feverish digging, carrying and lifting, as construction began on a new adventure camp site.

We would spend a month messing about in the jungle, getting a suntan, making friends, seeing wildlife such as buffalo, monkeys and even panthers, swimming and canoeing in the lake and singing worship songs around the camp fire. The price to pay for this was blood, sweat and blisters from the hard physical labour of laying foundations and digging in water pipes.

It would take us a day and a half to complete our journey from the coast to the hills so naturally we wanted to get moving. In India we discovered that no one works to a schedule so we just had to wait. Finally at eleven thirty, as we were about to give up and go to bed, our truck roared into the camp centre, and pulled up outside Cornerstone House, where we lived with the Gilbert family and the other Action Aiders (AAs).

Cornerstone is a guest house on the site and provides a place for tired missionaries, SU workers and others to rest and relax for a few days. Families often stay to enjoy the relaxed atmosphere of life by the sea. A two-minute walk takes you past the main buildings through the mango groves and palm trees, across the volleyball and football pitches (dug by AAs), through the glade of pine trees and the adventure playground (built by AAs) and out onto the beach. Here you can swim in the sea, sunbathe, walk along to Mahabalipuram, or just relax and look at the fishing boats and watch the waves as they roll endlessly off the Indian Ocean. I had arrived in India expecting to rough it and so to find myself staying in a place like this was a wonderful surprise. To come from central Leeds to this place, on my first trip abroad, occasionally had me wondering if I was dreaming. I really felt as though it was God who had put me there.

The driver and his two mates jumped out of the cab. We went out to meet them, relieved that loading would finally start. Our driver had other ideas.

'*Chai*?' he asked.

'You're joking! You keep us waiting all day and now you want a cup of tea! No chance!'

An enthusiastic display of sign language followed, backed up with Tamil phrases, which we did not understand, and bits of Tamil-style English, which we could just about follow. We soon gathered that they did not just want a cup of tea, they wanted a full slap-up meal. And they were not going anywhere until they got it!

The three friends climbed into the front of the truck and Paul and I got into the back. We drove half a mile and stopped by a roadside café serving *idlis* (rice cakes) and curry. While they consumed dozens of *idlis* and gallons of *chai*, eating about three times as much as an Englishman, we went round the stores that remained open and stocked up on biscuits and chocolate for the journey.

The high street was lined with all sorts of small shops: grocers, bakers, welders, chemists, tailors but no supermarkets or chain stores. Everything you could possibly want was sold in these tiny cramped shops. The lights from the open stores lit the dusty road outside. The road into Mahabalipuram is crammed with small hotels and souvenir shops. Along the side streets are the stone carvers who sit in their little thatched stalls chipping away producing elephants, turtles and idols. The larger statues are for temples and museums all over India. Tourists buy the smaller pieces. On the beach are the ancient Shore Temple and the Five Rathas. People have been carving stone in this area for centuries.

The night was warm. We were still in shorts and T-shirts at midnight. The hottest part of the year was approaching, when temperatures reach up to forty-five degrees. Up at Avalanche, though, it would be much cooler with plenty of rain to make us English feel at home.

When the meal was over we jumped back onto the truck and returned to the camp centre to load up. Piles of bricks, tiles and pipes, tents, canoes and paddles, and four big oil drums, stuffed with a million miscellaneous items, were to be loaded. On top of that would be our rucksacks and on top of them – us.

'You, there,' said our driver, gesturing towards us. 'No space!'

'Well, there must be a little. We have to go with you. We'll be all right.'

The driver shook his head, obviously a bit concerned for these crazy young men. However he realised we were determined so we got on with loading the stuff.

While we were passing tiles along a line to the truck, I remembered that deadly saw-scaled vipers lived around here. They stay in cool places in the day and come out from their hiding places at night. What better hiding place than a pile of tiles! By the time we had scared ourselves half to death imagining snakes under every tile it was time to tackle the rest of the stuff. We said our goodbyes, climbed onto the laden truck and lurched off into the dark night.

There was no other traffic on the road as we bounced over potholes and tried to get comfortable enough to sleep. We sat with our legs hanging over the tailgate, leaning back on the materials behind us. I was able to put my sleeping mat down and curl up in a tiny spot with my feet propped against the tailgate. Sharp bits dug into me and made sleep difficult. Every time I seemed to nod off we would hit a pothole which sometimes made up most of the road. It was a case of zzz... ow! ... zzzz... oof! Paul could only sit up straight and concentrate on not falling out of the truck. He always got the raw deal. While I was in excellent health, Paul had managed to get all sorts of cuts, bruises and stomach bugs.

Paul and I were by now best mates. We had met at Heathrow airport for the first time along with Jo (later known as Jo Girl). Although we were three very different people we all gelled together well, which was a good job. No one wants to spend two nights stuck on the back of a truck with someone

19

they do not like! Together we had dug a football pitch in the sand, built fences, run kids' clubs and all kinds of other things.

And so we sped on through the moonlit countryside of rural India. We watched the sun rise over the rice and wheat fields. We waved as we overtook an ox-cart laden high with straw. The driver's dark leathery face broke into a toothless grin as he waved back.

I nodded off to sleep again and when I woke two hours later the sun was high in the sky and we were stuck in a traffic jam. Occasionally someone blew their horn in frustration. Indians are very attached to their horns. They are required to blow them whenever they meet anyone else on the road and the larger the vehicle the louder the horn. We were deafened by blasts from lorries following us. Signalling at the drivers to stop it only seemed to make them worse but then blasting it in our faces was probably quite amusing to them as they sat nicely insulated in their cabs.

After two hours crawling along we finally went past the site of an accident, two dead cows sprawled out across the road. No one was making any attempt to move them. Cows are, of course, sacred to Hindus and to harm them is the worst possible crime against the gods. India is wrapped up in superstition and fear of bad spirits. Trucks are painted with scary faces to ward off evil spirits. People carry around little icons of gods which they hope will protect them from danger. Christianity really is a light in the darkness in this atmosphere. A God of love and forgiveness is a new concept to many. In a country where life can be very harsh, with little security against ill health, inability to work and so on, people have no option but to trust their god. As a Christian one hopes to show them something of Jesus.

White people are considered to be Christians, whether they are or not. Most of the white people in India are tourists, many of whom take drugs, fail to respect the local culture, through inappropriate dress for instance, and are often seen as contributing to problems such as child prostitution. This is some record for the Christians to try to combat! Simply through not drinking alcohol or smoking 'grass' we could be seen as different from the usual westerners. One drug seller in particular was absolutely incredulous that we did not want to buy his wares. 'You are English, yes? You no want grass? Good grass! Good grass!' We firmly resisted and left him shaking his head in disbelief.

A short distance down the road we saw another accident where a bus had come off the road. Then it was a truck that had ploughed through a wall. We decided to start counting and came across about another twelve accident scenes during our journey. We nearly caused one ourselves. A busload of people came up behind us, with the driver and those in front waving cheerfully. I got out my camera and as the bus was pulling out to overtake I took a photo. The driver of the bus smiled and showed us his best side, failing to keep his eyes on the road. We winced as the bus suddenly swerved back onto our side of the road to miss an approaching tractor by inches.

We could only guess how many people were injured in these accidents. India has an appalling road safety record as I saw for myself more than once. One day I was in a tiny tailor's shop in Mahabalipuram. As I looked at bright fabrics I heard shouting in the street and the squealing of tyres. I turned and saw a medium-sized lorry careering towards the shop entrance. A small girl had been hit and was bouncing along in front of the truck. I turned away as it smashed into the narrow entrance with a crunch. Glass flew around my legs and when I looked up the lorry was wedged in the doorway. The driver had made a run for it, fearing an angry mob, and he was nowhere to be seen. A bystander grabbed the girl who fortunately had got only a broken arm. The tailor and I climbed over the mangled bonnet of the truck into the street, feeling very relieved to have escaped serious injury by a matter of six feet. The Gilberts' moped was not so lucky. It was parked outside the shop and got literally flattened.

We pulled in at a roadside café for breakfast of *raita* and curry served on a banana leaf, as much as you could eat for fifteen rupees, which is less than thirty pence. Across the road was a well in a field where we washed ourselves.

We sunbathed on the back of the truck as we sat

watching the countryside shoot past – yellow and green fields, woods, small villages with their wooden huts and thatched roofs. We saw small kids bullying a scruffy dog, donkeys laden high with bricks, straw and all kinds of things were being led along the road. We listened to our Walkmans as we travelled. The sound of Jamiroquai and REM was perhaps a bit of a culture clash with our surroundings!

The landscape changed from the flat plains and we could see the Nilgiri Hills looming up. We began to climb up the valley towards our base at Ooty. Endless hairpin bends took us up through the jungle and then through the tea plantations. Monkeys lined the road, staring sternly at passing vehicles. There had been various landslides along this road and it was obvious that some rebuilding had taken place. We preferred not to think about what might happen if we hit a fresh landslide!

Sometime after midnight we made it to Ooty, a hill station for the British in the days of the Raj. Here we met up with Rod and Ruthie Gilbert and were able to catch up on some sleep before the last part of the journey to Avalanche. This involved among other things pushing a lorry uphill through mud, for more than a mile in the middle of the night in pouring rain.

For me going to India was a privilege. My time was packed full of experiences and discoveries about myself, and about God and his faithfulness. It was a chance to see the world from a new perspective. I cannot ever fully explain what India is really like. You would have to visit yourself to find out.

It was a time when my character really broadened out. I felt far more self-confident and capable on my return to England. Most importantly I learned far more about God and his faithfulness than in a lifetime of going to church. To live in a strongly Christian atmosphere, to meet people from the slums of Madras, with whom I had nothing in common but a faith in Jesus, built a feeling of security in God that was completely new to me. Reading the Bible properly for the first time was fascinating. Over that six months I felt a clear change of attitude away from simply doing whatever I pleased towards trying to please God through my lifestyle. God is powerful and trusting in him is the best anyone can do. No one should let doubts about what they are letting themselves in for put them off going abroad to work. It is a fantastic way to spend a year out!

Cowshed showers and blocks of ice

Name:	Rachael Scott
Organisation:	Bodybuilders, now called Soultime
Destination:	Watford, England
Mission:	to broaden in the Christian faith in every way through teaching and practical assignments

After finishing school I spent six months on the 'Bodybuilders' course run by Soul Survivor, Watford church. The title is rather misleading as it had got nothing to do with lifting weights and fitness training but was a 'discipleship training school'. Along with twenty-three other young people who were also on the course, I went off to live in a house in Watford. This might not sound that exciting but it is amazing how much you can learn based in Watford!

The course included one theology lecture a

week, a visiting speaker each week and a lot of practical community-based work. I had thought it would be fairly easy but I found some aspects of the time quite difficult. Although it was an amazing time and I am really glad I did it, there was plenty to challenge me.

We quickly discovered that twenty-four people do not always see eye to eye. This is especially true early in the morning when you have to queue for the shower. Being an only child I had never really had to share anything before, especially a bedroom, but I soon got used to it and now I really miss my room-mate. Everyone was friendly and, once we had got used to each other, it was fantastic.

There was always someone to chat with, to moan to or shout at, depending on what sort of day you had been having. There was an unending supply of people to go out and socialise with. The group was very good at practical jokes although fortunately I was not on the receiving end of some of the worst ones. The funniest was when the course leader walked in holding Daniel's boxer shorts which someone had managed to freeze into a block of ice. As the weather got warmer we developed a taste for water fights. One word of advice, learned the hard way: it is not a good idea to throw a bowl of water over anything electrical especially when one of the leaders catches you and is not amused!

Although we had lots of fun, some aspects of the course were hard for me. This was most noticeable in the things I had never done before, like public speaking – the most scary thing I have ever had to do in my entire life! Afterwards I realised it was definitely worth doing it. I am still not convinced that it was definitely worth doing all the essay writing. Even though our leaders said it was helpful for us, I found it plain boring. So did the rest of the Bodybuilders but I do not think many people expect to write essays as part of their gap year.

The hardest thing for me was working at the summer festivals. Soul Survivor runs Christian youth events every summer and as a Bodybuilder you get to work at all of them. It was great to be part of what was going on and to see what God was doing. However, living in a tent in the middle of a field for three weeks was not my idea of fun. It was particularly testing for me to have to try to shower in what I believe were ex-cowsheds. At times I felt as if God had deserted me but I survived and through it all learned a lot about depending on God.

As you may have gathered, all these hard things stretched me a lot. This meant I had to rely totally on God for just about everything. It can be hard and amazing at the same time. A couple of my favourite activities were the one day a week I spent working at a centre for adults with learning difficulties – I really loved that and it was always fun. The other favourite was the times we spent together as a group in prayer and worship.

There were plenty of more relaxing times too, like the day we went to Alton Towers and had to leave at six in the morning. Also the crazy idea to have a footballathon from four in the morning to ten at night. I must admit I did not actually play but it was fun to watch everyone else getting completely exhausted. I think that occasion created more injuries than all the other events put together. I have never seen so many twisted knees and ankles, strains and blisters.

Although I was doing a lot of practical things, the course actually had a huge effect on my faith. We spent lots of time in prayer and worship together and were encouraged to spend time alone with God as well. I was constantly being challenged about my beliefs and opinions. Bodybuilders provided the perfect opportunity for me to start sorting out some of these issues. My relationship with God grew and developed as I learned to depend on him more and had to trust him completely in different situations.

One of the most important things I learned was that God can provide me with all the things I need. It is what *he* thinks that matters, his opinion, and I should be living to please him and not just to please other people. I got into the habit of spending some time with God each day and it was much easier to do this on the course when I did not have the pressure of studying, or of being out at work. The more time I spent with him, the more I learned about his character and the more intimate our relationship became.

Setting aside six months to do this course was the best thing I could have done. It is tough having to deal with stuff and let God start changing you into the person he wants you to be. It is exciting to see God work and it is certainly worth it. Of course I have not stopped changing now. Just because I finished Bodybuilders does not mean that my relationship with God is totally sorted. However I have definitely moved forward and am in a much stronger place to be at university. I am trying to make my everyday life line up with what I believe.

I would advise everyone at least to consider taking a gap year before further education or full-time work. There are so many options available that there is probably something to suit everyone. Some people might have one thing they really want to do whereas others might want to keep their options open. Do not be put off by course descriptions and think, 'I could never do that!' Sometimes there is no real point in doing something you are very good at. We are all more capable than we think and God can help us when it is difficult. I know. I am the shyest person in the world when it comes to standing up before an audience but, with God's help, I managed to speak in front of a whole churchful of people.

I gained immensely from taking a year out. I made some excellent friends for life. I increased in confidence and moving away from home gave me a chance to grow up a bit before going to university. Most importantly I moved on a huge amount in my relationship with God. It was the maddest, wildest, hardest, easiest, most fun and best spent six months of my life so far!

Midsummer Night's Dream machine

Name:	Rosie Solly
Organisation:	Activate YFC
Destination:	all over Britain
Mission:	to present the gospel in a relevant way to young people using performing arts

I was in the Upper Sixth Form when I had my audition for Activate. Although I had been waiting for this audition for two years I did not understand fully what I would be doing if I was successful. I knew it would involve the creative arts and God, a combination that interested me a lot. The audition went well and I joined the team.

On the first of September I travelled to a centre to begin six weeks of rehearsals, training and teaching. I soon began to realise what Activate was about and to enjoy myself more and more.

Activate is a creative arts team run by a branch of Youth for Christ. I was in a team with fourteen other people and our main aim was to present the gospel in a relevant way to young people in Britain. The company has a two-part production which is based on *A Midsummer Night's Dream*.

The first part was performed many times to different year groups in a particular school. The second part was usually performed on a Friday night when the young people could choose whether they wanted to come or not. The play was packed with the latest chart songs and included ten dances, in which all the team took part. The play has the theme of relationships and we were able to take this subject and explore it in school Religious Education lessons. We also put on dance and music workshops, Christian Union meetings and youth events as well as church services.

Not surprisingly we were always on the go. At times this was hard because it was physically demanding and challenging. We would sometimes get up at six to set up in a school for morning assembly and would not leave the school until after five in the afternoon. In that time we might have done four performances, some lessons and a show.

Despite being so busy I can really say it was worth it as I met so many people and built friendships with people from all over Britain. My mates on the team were absolutely brilliant. We were with each other all year. Often we stayed together in people's homes near where we were performing and that helped us get to know each other well. It might sound cheesy but I think they are the best friends I have. They have seen me at my best and my worst, and witnessed my most embarrassing moments.

One of my favourite memories is of going to Spring Harvest and helping in the 14–16s venue and leading the after-hours events. The team had wanted to go there for months and we were really pleased when we were finally asked. I had a great time and I had lots of opportunities to perform with the team and also to chat with the young people attending the events.

One night at Spring Harvest one of my friends from Activate got up to dance on the stage while the band played. Nothing that unusual it would seem, but to me it was amazing. She had had a very bad knee with a torn cartilage, was on crutches for a time, was waiting for an operation and obviously could not dance. As a team we had prayed for her knee and she was healed. When I saw her dance it was so great. She was doing the thing she loved to do. Some of the young people at the event got up and danced behind her and worshipped God in their own way. It was great to see.

Although we worked hard it was a lot of fun and there was a great deal of laughter. I kind of miss being woken up by the minibus sounding its horn because it was time to leave for a school. I even miss getting dressed in a rush and trying to do my hair and make-up for a performance in the back of a moving vehicle.

The end of each week in a school was the time I most enjoyed Activate. It was not because I was leaving the school but because I had had the privilege of seeing God at work during the time we had been there. Many young people asked questions and responded to the message of the gospel. That was important to us and as a team we worked hard to make that possible and for me it made each week worthwhile and special. We would chat and pray with anyone who wanted to know more. During the week we were able to build up some good relationships with the pupils and I enjoyed that.

I must admit that standing up in front of a class was nerve-racking but always a laugh. We played games and mixed the learning with fun. Activate's lesson plans were very well organised so that a smaller group of four or five of us could take a class. In this way we could take several classes between us at the same time.

Whenever there was a chance of going out somewhere after work we took it. One freezing day we spent the whole time on a beach playing games, while a few of us who were mad went for a swim. Some of us spent a week with one host who had a swimming pool. We used the pool as much as possible and then got colds afterwards.

We had lots of friendly rivalry between the girls and the lads. The girls were very good at winding the lads up; they would deny this of course. On one occasion three of us were in a boat on a river and one of the lads got into a canoe. Warfare was declared, we all got soaked and had to swim to safety. This was rather difficult as we got stuck in the mud. The rest of the team shouted what I think they meant to be encouragement at us and we laughed until we ached.

The team met each week to pray for each other and whatever we would be doing in the next few days. We all valued and appreciated this. To help us keep focused on God we had regular times of Bible study.

The play itself was great and very funny. I was still laughing at the jokes after half the year had passed. By the time the first term had gone, everyone knew everyone else's lines. It became a lot harder to cover up mistakes without someone laughing at you as you went backstage.

It was a really great year and I would recommend it to anyone who has a heart to see young people get to know God better.

Although I missed everyone back home, I gained so many friends travelling around the country doing the things I love best.

Before I went on Activate lots of people said to me that it would be a life-changing experience. I did not understand what they meant until recently as I have had time to think back over the year. I feel that I value my faith a lot more. I can understand better where people's views and beliefs come from. I appreciate the different talents that people have and I am more creative in the way I use mine.

It was brilliant to spend a year with a bunch of great people who share the same passion and belief

as I do. I gained a lot from Activate, both spiritual-
ly and emotionally and feel I would not be where
I am now if it was not for the year I spent with
Youth for Christ.

I miss the team so much, but know we will stay
in touch.

Cooking, climbing and conversation

Name:	Dan Price-Davies
Organisation:	Abernethy Trust
Destination:	Inverness-shire, Scotland
Mission:	to demonstrate Christ's love through helping in the running of an outdoor activity centre

I first found out about the Abernethy Outdoor Centre from my dad who had led a Crusader group there about twenty years ago. I knew that I wanted to take a year out after school and before I did anything else, mainly because I wanted a break from studying. An outdoor centre was an obvious choice as I have been mountain walking and climbing since I was seven when my parents first took me with them into the hills.

When I was deciding where to go for my gap year I realised that I still wanted to work in the mountains but even more important to me was that I wanted to serve Jesus. The Abernethy Trust is a

Christian Outdoor Centre so it seemed the perfect place to apply for. I had a two-day interview in February of my last year at school. For most of these two days I worked in the kitchen and in the house, where all gap students work. I had two interviews, one with the In-House manager and one with the Big Boss. They put me at my ease as they were really informal and I got the impression that they were interviewing me to get to know me not just as a potential employee but more as a friend. I really loved the place so when I was offered a job I accepted it straight away.

I started work in the middle of August as one of the first new people to arrive. The others came towards the end of the month. The six of us who were taking the gap year would live, work and socialise together for the whole time. Fortunately we all got on well. The Trust try to match a group of people who look as if they might get on well, so if you are interested do not worry about whether or not you will make friends.

Normally we would start work at seven thirty in the morning and do an eight-hour shift. This was split into two parts if you worked in the kitchen as you worked mornings, had the afternoon off and worked again in the evening over dinner. If you were on the In-House team, as it was called, shifts were much more complicated so some days I did not start work until midday or even as late as mid-afternoon.

The work itself is not difficult but it took all of us

a few months to get the hang of things and work quickly and efficiently without having to ask what to do next. Apparently that is the same every year. I found working in the kitchen great fun as I had never done anything like it before. We were always telling jokes and funny stories and had lots of laughs.

When you are not working you can chill out and do nothing at all or you can join in anything that is going on, and there is always plenty to choose from. You get one and a half days off a week and on those days you can take part in whatever the groups are doing. Activities range from climbing to sailing, gorge walking to adventure courses. This was a great way to discover new sports, to get excellent instruction from work colleagues who were rapidly becoming your friends and, best of all, it costs nothing at all! You can do as much or as little as you like but I would definitely recommend taking part in some of the activities.

At first I just joined in with whatever group was there but as I got to know the other staff members I started going out with them on my days off so we could 'do our own thing' and get away from everybody else. Climbing is my main passion and about once a week I would climb with Simon who is the maintenance engineer.

There are about thirty staff at the Centre and of course all are different and have varied personalities. It was not always possible to get on well with someone. At times I felt very claustrophobic because I was living and working with the same people all the time. It was not that I did not enjoy my work but I needed to get a bit of time on my own away from the Centre. Sometimes I would go for a walk on my own for a couple of hours and spend part of that time talking to God. I came to the conclusion that it is natural to want to spend a bit of time by yourself and also to spend time alone with God. I think this would be true for me in any situation and it was something I learned about myself during my year out. For me it made the time better.

I loved all the attractions of living at Abernethy: the sports, the beautiful surroundings, earning some money and living away from home. However, more important to me than all of these attractions is knowing Jesus, who was and is my real passion. He is the reason I am alive and I know I will have eternal life through him. Being at Abernethy taught me such a lot about myself and my faith in Jesus. I learned how important it is to have a quiet time when I could read my Bible, think and pray, not just occasionally, but every day. I found out how important prayer is and that it works. I found that if I trusted God and obeyed him he would honour and bless me. I gained a new passion for Jesus which made me want to run out and tell everyone about him and about how much he loves us. In reality I was a little bit more reserved!

I have made life-long friends who share the same passion and enthusiasm and love for Jesus that I do.

The best bit is that I will know them for ever as we will all be in heaven together!

Working at the Centre is totally different from most other jobs. It is unique and totally amazing. The atmosphere is so friendly and it is great taking part in the events laid on for the guests. There is a real opportunity to get to know lots of new people, both staff and guests, from all sorts of different backgrounds.

Sometimes there were bad times when it felt as if nothing was going right and God seemed far away. I found that the only thing I could do then was to sit down and have a chat with God, tell him what was going on and ask him to help. My experience was that he did this more than I could have possibly imagined.

I loved my year out and I learned so much. I really miss being there but I can praise God for the amazing friends that he has given me and praise him for the brilliant work the Centre does.

You can be part of that too!

Breakfast of bad jokes

Name:	Bek Wharin
Organisation:	Abernethy Trust
Destination:	north of Cairngorm mountains, Scotland
Mission:	helping practically in running a Christian outdoor centre

I had decided to take a year out and I wanted to spend the time doing something that would be a real challenge and experience and where I would meet people whom I could develop some great friendships with.

Unknown to me a place called Abernethy Outdoor Centre was advertising for staff who would be willing to spend a year working in the highlands of Scotland. The sort of people they wanted were those who would be willing to serve others and learn the meaning of servanthood and humility. I had never been near the place or even heard of it.

As far as I was concerned, I was going to have a stunning year teaching English in Nepal then going trekking. Through what seemed to be a chance meeting (I don't think!) with a friend of a friend I found out about Abernethy and that they had a vacancy on their house-team. They made the Centre sound fantastic, which it is, and two weeks after first hearing about the place I was on my way for an interview. After a long train journey up to Nethy Bridge I found there was a me-shaped vacancy that I could not ignore. So I accepted the job.

Even by this time I had already begun to learn that God had a place that was just perfect. His plan for me was so much better than mine was. I knew I had lots of things in my life that were far from perfect but even I could see that Abernethy was where God wanted me to be.

The job involved working in the house generally or in the kitchen. Wherever I worked had its ups and downs. However from the start you get the idea that this is a good time to start to put your own needs second and to make it your priority to keep Abernethy running smoothly. Of course by the time I realised this, the place was my home.

Working with a team of young Christians is a good experience. You know that primarily you are all there to serve God. It only took me a couple of weeks to feel settled. I think this was because you all live and work at such close quarters that your fellow workers become like a family.

The centre is one of four run by the Abernethy Trust. All kinds of groups visit for a time of out-door activities. Mainly the groups were not Christians. This means that the centre has a unique opportunity to tell hundreds of people about God in an environment where we also have the chance to demonstrate something of his love as well.

In the evenings there are 'time-out' meetings and we helped with them. For school parties we would usually sing a couple of songs all together, maybe have a quiz, a short talk and some discussion and interaction with each other. The aim was to give the kids a glimpse of what God meant to us as staff and why he was significant to us personally. For many this was the first time they had come across this sort of thing.

From one short year I have a stack of memories of these meetings. Sometimes people made their own open commitment to God. Sometimes guests learned a little bit more about Jesus and what he is like. At times there was a lot of contact with the guests during the day, such as when we were serving them food, or when they were wandering around the house and gardens.

One thing I definitely learned is that the more you put into a situation the more you get out of it. Just to get through a long shift in the kitchen is not enough! There are endless opportunities to get to know the guests and be involved in their pro-gramme. To do this, though, involves supernatural energy, and there is only one place to get that!

I gained so much from my year at Abernethy after the initial shock of getting used to starting work at half past seven in the morning, looking after myself and being away from home. Living in a Christian community, although claustrophobic at times, was fantastic because I got to know some absolutely top people there. It is really great to be able to work with such a wide range of characters who all have the same basic desire to serve God. At Abernethy the staff come from all over Britain, and some from all over the world. During the year you are very unlikely to feel lonely as there are at least thirty staff around all the time.

The centre is just north of the Cairngorm Mountains and it has just about every facility you could wish for in an outdoor centre. Personally I took advantage of the free squash and mountain biking more than anything else, but there were loads more activities on offer. My home town is in the Midlands and I found it immensely cool to be in the wilds of Scotland for a year. You can walk out of the Centre and see a range of mountains reaching four thousand feet. I found looking at these always helped to put things in perspective.

All our food was provided and I soon got used to a full cooked breakfast every morning at nine o'clock. This was a fun half hour when the team ate together, had a short rest, groaned at the bad jokes and made comments about the wonderful variety of table manners on show. It was always a highlight of the day.

During the winter there are opportunities to snowboard, ski downhill or cross-country and generally enjoy the heavy snowfalls. Snowball fights became an essential after-work activity and we found some serious sledging sites close to the Centre.

In the summer there is an influx of unaccompanied young people at the Centre and a greater freedom for staff to get to know them well. As a member of staff you get loads of chances to take part in the band, as a group leader, in interviews and whatever is going on. I found that in the meetings I helped in, God gave me a confidence that I do not normally have. My advice to anyone working for their gap year at Abernethy is to jump in at the deep end with the youth work. It is great!

There are other ways of spending a year at the Centre if you do not want to be on the house-team. Some work is available in maintenance or at other centres as a trainee instructor.

More than any time in my life up to now I experienced such strong friendship and fellowship with people at Abernethy and this has benefited me so much. Obviously I missed home at times. Working five and a half days on the trot did become tiring but I can honestly say that it was the best year of my life yet.

My favourite activities are outdoor pursuits. Abernethy uses these and the hospitality and friendship they offer to glorify God. It is an exciting place to work. I had loads of fun with water fights and parties and endless funny incidents that made us roll round on the floor laughing until our stomachs hurt. The friends I made will be friends for life.

More than all this, though, this was the first time I have given a year to God. I learned so much about him and about myself. This was a time for him, to work hard whether on duty or not, knowing he was by my side whatever I was doing.

Back on the road again

Name:	Beth Redman
Organisation:	TVB Band, Youth for Christ
Destination:	Britain, Croatia
Mission:	to communicate the good news about Jesus to young people through music

When I was eighteen my life was turned around when I became a Christian on an Oak Hall skiing holiday. From that moment God really began to get hold of my life. I started reading my Bible and praying that God would give me a purpose and that he would use me.

Soon after, a friend sent me a verse from the Bible that encouraged me that God had been hearing my prayers.

It is Jeremiah chapter 29 verses 11 to 14 and it says, 'For I know the plans I have for you,' declares the Lord, 'plans to prosper you and not to harm you, plans to give you hope and a future. Then you will call upon me and come and pray to me, and I will listen to you. You will seek me and find me when you seek me with all of your heart. I will be found by you,' declares the Lord.

One day, as I began to read these verses and pray, I felt God tell me really clearly that I was going to work with young people and in particular in schools. This surprised me, as my schooldays were the worst days of my life. I suffered terrible bullying for most of my time at secondary school. My parents were splitting up and home life was pretty awful in general. Most days I would get my school uniform on and just hang around at the back of the shops too afraid to go to school, completely lonely and with what appeared to be 'no hope and no future'.

God began to remind me of my schooldays and one day I remember so clearly it was as if I could see an assembly hall filled with eight hundred faces. It was my face eight hundred times over! I felt as if God was saying to me, 'What would you say to that girl now?' My head was spinning with all the things I should have loved to have known back then. Things like there is a God who loves me, who died for me. That I am important, someone loves me and God has plans for me. Suddenly it became clear I really wanted to go into schools and tell people like me about Jesus, tell them what I had so needed to hear back then – but how?

I prayed and prayed that God would give me an opportunity and open the doors for me.

My hobby at that time was singing in a group

called 'Speak Easy', a Christian band. We performed mainly in pubs and clubs but occasionally at Christian events. It was at Spring Harvest, a Christian Easter holiday-cum-conference, that I heard about Youth for Christ and in particular about TVB.

TVB is a ten-piece band comprising a drummer, a bass player, lead guitarist, two keyboards, saxophone, three singers and a sound engineer. TVB is mostly a covers band doing the latest songs from the charts and also some Christian stuff. They spend an average of ten months travelling around secondary schools in the UK and Europe taking lessons, assemblies, Christian Unions and lunchtime concerts. They use the music to attract young people and as a way to tell people about Jesus.

I applied to the band and within two months I was accepted. The only thing I needed to do was to raise three and a half thousand pounds. The money is needed to cover the costs of sending a band on the road with lighting, vans, equipment, costumes etc.

I sold my car and got three people to sponsor me regularly. Eventually, through people's ongoing support, all the money came in!

Anyway that is enough of an introduction. Let's get down to the nitty-gritty. I arrived at the Youth for Christ training camp on the ninth of September excited, fired up and ready for action. The training camp was an intense four-week experience where all the different YFC gap year projects get together for training, rehearsals and preparation. If anything was going to knock the stuffing out of a bunch of over-keen teenagers it was training camp!

I had not thought I had signed up for four weeks of long working days, constant rehearsals and a lot of discipline! I was quite thankful when the camp was over and we could all get down to the stuff we had come for.

An average week ran something like this. On Sunday night we would arrive at our host church for a debriefing and a piece of cake. By seven in the morning on Monday we would have started setting up in a local school so as to be ready for assembly. Then we would do a day of Religious Education lessons before going back to our host's home for tea. The next day, Tuesday, we would do the same thing at another school, maybe add in a lunchtime concert, and so it went on every day of the week. Church activities or group meetings could also be part of the day. By Friday evening we had been in most of the town's secondary schools and told hundreds of young people about Jesus.

On Friday night we held a concert for an hour. Many of the young people we had contacted during the week would turn up to this gig. There would be a ten-minute talk and any who were interested in finding out more about Jesus would come and chat to us.

Some weeks we would see more than eighty teenagers coming forward to get to know Christ.

TVB was always linked with a local church and it was essential that we knew people would care for those who had made commitments during our time with them.

On Saturdays we could chill out and collapse and then we would move on to the next place and start all over again.

For me there was nothing better than peeping out from behind the stage curtain and seeing a room full of young people, knowing that some of them would soon become Christians. It was an amazing privilege to be part of something so fruitful and exciting.

During the year we travelled all over Britain, from Devon to Scotland. We also went to Croatia, one of the highlights of the year for me. We stayed at a place called 'The Life Centre'. This had been set up in a house to accommodate many young people who were mostly orphans and who had fled from Bosnia. Although we could not speak the same language it was amazing to have contact with such brave young people. They were not bitter towards God despite their horrific experiences.

There is no way I would have been able to meet people like these or to travel so extensively if I had not joined YFC for my gap year.

I came into the team full of zeal and enthusiasm but also incredibly rebellious and strong-willed. Doing TVB forced me to change and to cling on to God and to depend on him in a way I had never done before. It felt so healthy to be part of a diverse group of people, all with different personalities. I learned to work closely and to love people whom I would never normally have been friends with. It was a precious learning experience.

I would wholeheartedly recommend TVB, not because I think it was comfortable and cosy and fun – it often was not – but because it was where I grew up and began to learn what it really means to serve God.

A passage that sums it up for me is found in Matthew chapter sixteen and verse twenty-four: 'Then Jesus said to his disciples, 'If anyone would come after me, he must deny himself and take up his cross and follow me. For whoever wants to save his life will lose it, but whoever loses his life for me will find it.''

Who swallowed the light bulb?

Name:	Natalie Bayne
Organisation:	Crosslinks
Destination:	Republic of Ireland
Mission:	to help with children's Christian holiday camps

I went away for six weeks in the summer of 1998 as part of my gap year. It might have only been a short time but I thoroughly enjoyed it.

I was part of a team of eight people who went off to the Republic of Ireland with Crosslinks to work at Christian holiday camps. Each week we would take a church service and 'sell' the idea to the parish of what we would be doing. Then every morning from ten until one o'clock we would teach children aged from four to fourteen about Jesus. Each day we had a theme, a Bible story, some drama, a memory verse, quiz, craft, worksheet and games.

We could choose which age group to work with, so I tried them all. I found that the eight to tens were the most challenging for me. I soon learned that to work with children you have to believe fully what you are saying. Otherwise they see right through you. They also help you to see things from a different viewpoint. I can remember one day having a discussion with some six-year-olds on what we would say to Jesus if he turned up on our doorstep!

During those weeks I increased my own knowledge about Jesus and at the same time learned to simplify things so the children could understand better. I think we often make the Bible so complicated it is difficult for any of us to really grasp it.

I enjoyed the time we spent with the children. At Clonakilty in County Cork the team got on particularly well together. I looked forward to the quizzes to see whether the children had actually learned what we had been trying to teach them. We would ask them the memory verse, then see if they could remember the theme or maybe what a parable is. Every day we would have a fun time when they had to discover the answer to such questions as, 'Which team member has swallowed a light bulb?'

The children knew we were genuine about our faith because we were really enjoying our times with them. They could see that we cared for each other and for them and hopefully it gave them some insights into what it is like relating to other Christians.

I especially enjoyed taking the church service at the beginning of the week. During that time I think we were able to bring something of value to every member of the congregation. I believe that many adults were able to see their perception of Christianity change a little.

We all took part in the morning and evening prayer sessions every day. As I saw how this encouraged sharing and fellowship within the group it made me realise the value of small groups in a fresh way. We also had a youth night and a parents' night each week. These were pretty challenging and tough to do but did give us lots of opportunities to talk to people.

Each week we moved to a different town and often the team changed. Not many were as stupid as me and did five lots of holiday clubs. I found the first couple of days of each week hard because I had to get to know new people and start to develop new friendships. However by the end of the week we usually knew each other very well. I hope I will have many of the friends I made for life. I had imagined I would find it hard to understand people because of their different regional accents. In fact it was the opposite. People could not understand me. One team member told me that I sounded like Wallace out of Wallace and Grommit!

Although there was a lot of hard work we had time for many adventures. I have some funny memories of playing games in St. Stephen's Green in Dublin, much to the embarrassment of the local team members. I visited many beaches and, much to my surprise, it did not rain all the time. I was told that you can tell when it is summer in Ireland because the rain is warm! We had lots of laughs about our different accents and also about our wrong preconceptions of the Irish. We soon discovered that they do not all drink Guinness or have ginger hair.

Before I went, I thought my time with Crosslinks would be a simple matter of going to Ireland, working with the children and telling them about Jesus and then coming back home. End of story. It was not like that. I was struggling to decide what to study at University and during a time of group prayer a verse from Jeremiah impressed itself on me. In chapter twenty-nine and verse eleven it says, and it is God who is talking, "I have good plans for you, not plans to hurt you. I will give you hope and a good future."

This was not the only time I heard God speaking to me about something I was finding hard. I felt I had been given a new desire to learn about God. I could tell by the end of the six weeks that God had been with us all the time. We were kept safe and healthy and looked after by the parish, who each day gave us a meal. I realised that we are always ready to blame problems and trials on God, but we do not thank him enough when things are good.

I am particularly happy that I decided to take some time out before going to University. If I had not, I would not have had this chance for change. Whether it is at home or abroad I would really recommend that you go some place where you can develop your relationship with God. When you go away you have to become dependent on God. This is why this sort of work is so important. It forces you to learn a lot of things.

If God is in your co-pilot seat, swap places. Cheesy, but true.

Footie fans, baguettes and the hairy caterpillar

Name:	Helen Campbell
Organisation:	OM (Operation Mobilisation)
Destination:	Nantes, France
Mission:	street evangelism

Looking back I have not got a clue why I actually went. On the thirteenth of June 1998 I set off on a short-term mission for two weeks to Nantes in France. I was going with the organisation 'Operation Mobilisation' (OM) but that was about all I knew about the mission. I was seventeen years old and felt completely out of my depth.

When I arrived in France and met the other members of the team I was physically shaking, but it was not as bad as I thought it was going to be. If you are thinking about going on a mission, then just go before you talk yourself out of it! It was one of the most nerve-racking times of my life, especially at the start, but it turned out to be the best two weeks of my life. It was so good that I aimed to go back the next year.

There were about forty-five people in the team from all over the world. My time in France certainly changed my outlook on the world. We stayed on a campsite in tents and personally I found the tents the hardest part of the mission. It may sound funny to you but they stank, they were dirty and when I found a hairy caterpillar on my sleeping bag, that was the last straw. As I was sleeping next to the door of the tent, all my clothes got wet and muddy and often half my sleeping bag was sticking out of the end of the tent. So here are another couple of tips from one who knows! Tall people and small tents do not mix. If you are going on a mission and hear the word 'tent', book yourself into a nearby hotel.

We had a bus to take us around Nantes to our evangelism spots and once it crashed into a parked car. Well, just in case I have not totally put you off this sort of work, I will tell you the only other bad point about the time in France. Baguettes. I hate baguettes at the best of times, but with soggy cucumber…!

Right, now I have got that out of my system, I will move on to the good points about the mission. Firstly, the people I met on the team were the most wonderful people I have ever met. I did not feel out of place at all and, despite the mixed ages and cultures, the team got on really well together. I have never been in a group before where there has not been someone who has been left out, or someone who is the most popular. I had left school only two weeks before I went to France so I had thought everyone would be in the same situation as me. Obviously they were not, but the great thing was that everyone in the team was treated as an equal. It was like a big happy family and I can honestly say I got on well with every single person.

In the mornings we had breakfast around half past eight and then went to a church for a session where we prayed, had a time of worship and did some training for our evangelism. Then we had lunch at the restaurant at Nantes University. After that we had two or three hours to wander around or sunbathe. This gave me a good chance to show off my grasp of the French language since I got completely lost. You do not have to be able to speak another language to go on a mission, although it would be an advantage. To be honest my French is appalling and none of the French people could understand me at all.

At four in the afternoon we met in small groups to pray and we asked God to help us to meet people who would want to hear about Jesus as we went out into the town. Then the bus took us into the centre of Nantes. We took a packed tea (baguettes) and bags full of leaflets. I found this very scary. I felt a bit silly at first but I soon got into the swing of things. While the French-speaking members of the team went round with questionnaires to get people talking about God, I 'mass distributed' leaflets to passers-by and prayed for those that other team members were talking to.

The World Cup was on while we were there and the atmosphere was amazing! On the days that there were games in Nantes, I was able to meet quite a lot of people who spoke English. We gave out leaflets with the personal testimonies of some of the 1994 Brazil squad to football supporters, in all different languages, and we gave out copies of John's Gospel and of the Jesus videos to the people we talked with.

It was a wonderful experience to meet football supporters from all over the world and to be able to give them leaflets which told them that knowing God was even better than supporting their team. They were very friendly. I think it was World Cup excitement in the air! On our day off I managed to get tickets to see Chile versus Cameroon – another highlight of the trip.

I had some memorable moments talking to people. Two in particular stand out to me. I met an English football supporter who was a drug addict. While he was in prison he had given his life to Jesus but he now believed that God had given up on him. I talked with him and told him that God loved him. He took a John's Gospel and promised to read it. I have been praying for him ever since.

Another time I spent in focused prayer for two other team members who were having conversations nearby. Afterwards I found out that Dennis had been talking to a man he had met several years before. This man had told Dennis that he had always remembered him and the things he had told him about God all those years ago. The other person I had been praying for was so eager to hear about God that he became a Christian right then and there.

There were times when I felt like giving up and there were times when I thought I was wasting my time, but God worked through me in a way that I never thought he would. I had a wonderful time in France and know that my interest in mission work will not stop there. I feel really pleased that I gave so many people the chance to find out more about knowing God. You might not think you are 'Christian' enough to do missionary work. I thought I certainly was not, but I believe that God uses everyone who is willing to serve him. Maybe it will be through praying, or talking to people or giving out leaflets. Everyone on the team had different things to offer and God used every talent.

I do not think it matters if you cannot commit yourself to a life-long service as a missionary. I think God is delighted when we want to learn about mission, however much time we can give to it.

Breaking the language barrier through mime

Name:	Andy Parle
Organisation:	OM (Operation Mobilisation)
Destination:	Lisbon, Portugal
Mission:	various forms of outreach at Expo '98

I am Andy Parle and I live in Newbridge, County Kildare. When I was nine years old I became a Christian. While I was growing up I went to a Bible Club where we were taught well the truth of the Bible. We also listened to missionary stories and learned how the gospel was spread across the world.

There was a young man called Michael who used to visit our club. He became a close friend. He told us of his adventures as a missionary with Operation Mobilisation (OM). He had spent four years working as a radio operator on one of their ships. These ships, the Doulos and Logos II, travel the world and take the gospel wherever they go. Michael really enjoyed the work and his enthusiasm inspired me so that one day I wanted to join an OM team.

When I was seventeen I began to consider going on an outreach team during my summer break. I knew OM ran such things so I wrote off to their head office in England for information. At the same time I began to ask people for advice and they encouraged me to go for it.

Well, I chose to go to Lisbon in Portugal when the outreach would be at EXPO '98, a huge global event visited by thousands of people every day. I began writing letters to friends and churches asking for financial support. Everything started to fall into place and I was amazed to see how God provided everything I needed. This helped me to know that I was doing the right thing and that God was on my side.

On the twenty-fifth of July I arrived at the airport for my flight. Talk about Jesus' instruction to take up your bed and walk! That was just what I was doing. We had to bring everything! I had to bring a pillow, first-aid kit, torch, clothes line and pegs for my washing. I could have been going to darkest Africa!

The flight went well and I arrived safely at Lisbon airport. It was midday, the sun was shining and it was really hot. When I got into the arrival hall I looked around for someone with an OM poster. However when I had looked around for a long time I realised there had been some form of miscommunication between us. For several hours I was on my own. I tried to find the team I was supposed to join by going to the exhibition place and being helped by a policeman, taxi driver and bus driver. However I still could not work out where I should be. Eventually after some phone calls everything was sorted out and I met up with the right people. I must say that those few hours of uncertainty meant that I really had to trust God for what was going on. I felt very grateful to God that things worked out fine in the end, that I had not made any unwise decisions while I had been on my own and that God had kept me safe.

By the way my advice to anyone going off anywhere is to be sure of your emergency phone numbers and addresses!

I met up with the rest of the team and we spent the first week in training and preparation and getting to know each other. We were all from different countries. We stayed in a town just outside Lisbon called Chelas. The people were poor and there were children everywhere. I noticed a lot of stray dogs roaming through the town. We were accommodated in a church hall which was fairly basic but we managed well together.

During the next two and a half weeks we did most of our outreach at EXPO '98. After breakfast each morning and our quiet times with God, we went off in a rusty green van to give out tracts and to talk to people as they went into the exhibition. Over eighty thousand people from all over the world went there every day. This meant we had lots of opportunities to talk about Jesus. I went for the ones who spoke English, but the tracts were in many languages.

In the afternoon it was usually very hot. We would do odd jobs like cleaning, write letters or catch up on some sleep. By the evening we would be ready to go off again.

This is when we would split up and half the team would do children's work in the village, using mime and drama, song and sketch-board presentations of the gospel. The children were very noisy and wild but they loved hearing about Jesus.

The other half of the team would go back to EXPO '98 and do mimes, drama sketches and sing. I enjoyed the mimes best and have had opportunities to do some since I came home. Sometimes we went into Lisbon itself to do our outreach. I talked to many people and enjoyed telling them about Jesus and how he can save them and give them eternal life.

Overall the three and a half weeks were great. Sometimes it was tiring and frustrating but I knew Jesus was always with me to help me. The experience has made me more confident and stronger in my faith. I really recommend going on an outreach team, for any Christian who wants to grow. You learn more about yourself, your faith and about God who never leaves you nor forsakes you.

The miracle of the minibus at Milange

Name:	Hannah Bye
Organisation:	OM (Operation Mobilisation)
Destination:	Mozambique
Mission:	building work, helping with children's groups and church services

July the fourth 1998. I awoke to find tingles going up and down my spine. After months of planning I was finally going to Africa. Was I nervous? Of course! Though naturally self-confident, the idea of going to serve God in an unknown country was terrifying at the very least.

Final goodbyes were made at Heathrow and we soon discovered other members of our team. My bright striped trousers were a major identifying factor! The flight was uneventful but stepping out onto the land to which God had called me was an absolutely amazing experience. Our programme was to include a training week in South Africa followed by our work in Mozambique.

The first shock to the system was finding that we needed to get up at six in the morning. I am not a morning person and was quite unaware that anything could happen at this unearthly hour. I staggered to the kitchen to make a cup of tea, only to discover that it was South African and not particularly pleasing to my taste buds! Apart from this the food was great, the team got on well together and the teaching was incredible.

Probably the most important lesson I learned from my training week was the power of prayer. Our destination was Mocuba, North Mozambique, and the sheer size of our team would not allow us to take just one route. Deciding who was to go which way was not an easy decision. Thelma, our leader, encouraged us to go and pray about it. The idea was to come back with five names written down – these would go the more awkward route. God obviously moved in this situation, as many of our lists contained the same names.

Although most of the team were English, there were others from around the world. I went the easier route which included eight border crossings. Things went well until we tried to get into Malawi.

The majority of the team had no problem as EU citizens do not need visas. However Switzerland is not part of the EU and our Swiss member, Tabea, had no visa. No amount of persuasion could get her into the country and she had to go back to Zimbabwe with a friend. We found ourselves wondering why God would allow this to happen, forgetting that he always has a greater plan.

Meanwhile we carried on our journey, arriving at Milange, the border between Malawi and Mozambique. At this point we had not got the slightest clue how we were going to get to Mocuba. Transport of any kind is rare and no doubt we would have to split up again. Going through customs we watched as a minibus drew up. A new minibus! An empty, sixteen-seater minibus going in the same direction as us! A reasonable price was agreed and we found ourselves travelling in relative comfort! Who says that God does not do miracles now!

We were told to look out for the pink house just before Mocuba. 'Unmissable' was the phrase used. However as we went into the town it became obvious that we had missed it. We turned around, asked directions and found out that the pink house had been painted white only the previous week. Exhausted from our travelling, we quickly introduced ourselves and then headed for the tents.

There were already a number of long-term missionaries, mostly South African, working in Mocuba with OM. A lot of our work was to help them to build up good relationships with the local people. Also we were to serve them by doing some practical work.

The first morning we were thrown straight in at the deep end and set off to start our work. Instead of driving into town we had to walk. Many of the local people believed that as rich foreigners we were only interested in ourselves, so walking, like they had to, instead of driving, was part of our witness. I will never forget the children's faces. Every day they would run out to see us walking past, greeting us with their huge smiles and cheerful 'Bom dia' (good morning).

Mozambique is a beautiful country and turned out to be much greener than I had anticipated. There are palm trees everywhere, helping to make up the magnificent landscape. The country is poor, partly as the result of a recent civil war and landmines are a possibility. The houses were what I had expected with mud walls and thatched roofs. The people were happy despite old torn clothing and a hospital that was not very clean.

Two days after our arrival the rest of the team turned up. Much to our surprise so did Tabea. Our team leader had made a phone call which resulted in Tabea being met by a missionary in Zimbabwe and she had managed to get her visas in record time. God knew what he was doing after all. Our faith was built up by this experience.

We worked on the houses every morning, bonding, painting and fixing. It was hard work but then we had not gone there for a holiday. In the afternoons we visited the local people. It was very difficult to get out of our English mindsets and remember that the culture was completely different. We found, for example, that we were unwilling to go to a house if we had not been invited, yet this is seen as a great compliment. We spoke in a mixture of English and Portuguese using our phrase books to help. The local people found our attempts at their language quite amusing, especially my inability to pronounce the words for 'house' and 'trousers' differently.

Sundays were certainly the highlight of the week for me. We would be invited to various churches where we would be asked to take part. Normally four or five of us went to each church. We did all sorts of different things, depending on what our particular talents were. Most weeks I was able to speak while others gave testimonies, acted out drama sketches or we sang worship songs together.

The style of worship was amazing and included a lot of enthusiastic singing and dancing. We soon found that even those on our team with only a basic knowledge of the Bible often had been taught more than the church leaders.

For the second part of our time there we did children's work every other afternoon. This was really special to me as I loved working with the children. We played lively games with them, the idea being to use up their energy before the story. This turned out to be an impossible task! We then worked through some Bible stories, teaching them memory verses and singing songs.

We were also able to visit some local pastors. One day I came home and had my dinner. It was usually rice and bean stew, sometimes with chicken. Hannah, one of the other team members, then asked me to go to a pastor's house with her. I agreed and we set off, with me riding on the back of the pastor's bike. It was quite an experience as he would forget I was there and my legs banged into every possible obstacle. The first thing I saw in his house were two very large pots, one holding rice, the other bean stew. In the culture it was very bad to refuse food if you were offered it as it was like rejecting the person who had made the offer. My stomach was still full but I thought if I ate very slowly I would be okay and no one would press me to have a second helping. This plan did not work as we were there for a long time and before the evening was over I had five more generous helpings. I was so loaded with food I could hardly balance on the bike going home.

One of the things which really scared me before I went, was the thought of snakes and spiders. There were plenty of the latter. The one I remember vividly was near the end of our mission. We had a big youth conference and were taking it in turns to say something. While others were talking we would sit at the side of the church on mud lumps. Above our heads were decorations of vines strung across the rafters. While I was sitting I was suddenly aware of a bright yellow, furry spider above my head. I did not pay much attention to the rest of the meeting after that as I was too busy making sure the spider did not fall on me!

The trip was an experience of a lifetime and I would love to go back in the future. To anyone thinking of going on a mission, like I did with OM,

I would thoroughly recommend it. You will learn so much about God, others and yourself. There will be times when you feel like going home but God will always be there for you. Just do not take too many clothes and don't forget some Mars bars!

Sunsets, stars, stones and solitude

Name:	Julian Barnes-Darcey
Organisation:	Life Ministry
Destination:	Garissa, Kenya
Mission:	help in a school, use *Jesus* film as a means of outreach

In the summer of 1998 Garissa, an inconspicuous town in eastern Kenya was my home for a month. Garissa lies in the middle of the desert, hundreds of kilometres from any other civilisation. It is only a small town but it has plenty of character. The inhabitants are a mix of Kenyan and displaced Somalis with one characteristic in common: Islam. Unfortunately the town's appearance does not reflect this diversity. It is very plain with little charm or elegance and the limited number of buildings that do exist are mostly concrete bunga-lows. Once you are out of town though, you are confronted with a magnificent sight. In nearly every direction vast plains of awe-inspiring desert appear before you. Yet it is not all desert. On the edge of the town runs the river Tana. This is the home of many hippopotamuses and crocodiles. It also provides water for some thick vegetation to grow and this is a good place for monkeys to hide.

In order to reach Garissa it was necessary to take a six-hour bus journey from Nairobi, the capital of Kenya. It was quite an experience. The roads we travelled on were very basic with potholes everywhere. With a cautious driver this would not have been a problem but the bus drivers are all madmen. They race along these roads at incredible speeds, causing the buses to hurtle in and out of these holes and most people to be either afraid or feel sick, or, like me, both!

Once in Garissa I worked for a Christian organisation called The Life Ministry. This seeks to share the love of Christ with the Muslim community. All but one of its workers were Kenyan. I was the only westerner.

During my stay I was involved in many different activities. The principal one was helping out in a primary school established by Life Ministry. The aim was that they would be able to offer hope in the future to the children through Christ's love. The children in turn might impact the community. Local parents were prepared to send their children to this school as it was the best of the few that exist in the area. I helped out with small jobs around the school.

One thing that really struck me about the school was the friendliness of the children. All of them would come energetically to talk to me, especially when I pulled out my camera. They loved having their photos taken. What was so surprising about it was that these children were more friendly with foreigners than the rest of the community seemed to be. Adults would rarely speak to me in a friendly manner and, apart from the odd exception, refused to have their photograph taken. The children, however, seemed free from any prejudgments towards westerners.

Perhaps the most enjoyable experience was showing the film *Jesus* in the open air at night. This film is taken from Luke's Gospel and is about the life of Jesus. Several evenings a week we would venture out into the night, to various locations in and around Garissa, put up a projection screen and, using a generator, show the film to anyone who cared to watch. The film was translated into Swahili. It was hoped that seeing this film would turn people towards Christianity. One showing in particular remains firmly in my mind.

We went to show the film to some prisoners in a very small prison. It did not seem to be much more than a concrete hut. We were not allowed access into the prison so we put a screen near the outside fence and the prisoners watched it from the windows. It was on the journey home that things started to liven up. Driving in our jeep along the bumpy road in the silent dark night we were suddenly bombarded with stones. From all sides stones crashed into the car, the front windscreen was shattered. Fear instantly struck our hearts. Yet somehow we managed to keep on driving until we had passed beyond the reach of the stones. Thankfully no one was hurt. The people throwing the stones were probably angry that we were showing the film in an attempt to interest Muslims in Jesus.

Another poignant aspect of my stay was the realism of life. Naturally it was completely different from London. For instance I saw where all my food came from. When we ate chicken we would go to the chicken shed, pick one out, take it home, kill it, clean it, cook and eat it. The sincerity of the people was also a welcome change. All the Christians I met were extremely kind to me. They did everything they possibly could to make my stay a memorable one.

Even though it was winter there, coming from England I found the days very hot. Despite the fact that the sun did not shine every day it was always humid and by the time I left I was roasted. The days however were short. As Kenya is on the equator, darkness descended by seven every night. The sunsets though were startling. The sun would descend in a blaze of pink. The nights were also amazing. The air would become fresh and cool and most nights the sky would be clear, illuminated by thousands upon thousands of stars. Sleeping however was not always easy. Throughout the night the piercing screams of hyenas and the annoying groans of donkeys would echo through the crisp African air. At precisely four o'clock every morning a Muslim chant from the mosque would ring out, calling the people to prayer.

This was a particularly enriching time for me spiritually. Although I had a marvellous time there were occasions when loneliness would set in. Being the only westerner in the community could sometimes be hard. On these occasions though I found relief through reading my Bible. It comforted me enormously. This reliance on God brought me closer to him.

Seeing how the Life Ministry members devoted their lives to serving God was also a great influence and left a deep impression. On top of their work and church, which was full of African character, we had several Bible studies each week. Their passion for God rubbed off on me and made me stronger in my faith. I pray it may continue!

You need a sink? Have mine!

Name:	Georgina Bromwich
Organisation:	Latin Link
Destination:	Bolivia
Mission:	building construction, helping with church services

No one I know seems to know much about Bolivia. Unlike most South American countries it is not famous for football. It does not have the same reputation as Colombia for drugs or violent deaths (although my mum was worried when she first knew I wanted to go there). Even when I went to send a letter to Bolivia, the lady at the post office thought it was somewhere in the former USSR. I study geography but before going to work there I only knew vaguely where Bolivia was. Going was definitely the best way to find out about the place. I went for six weeks as part of the Latin Link Summer STEP project in 1998.

Bolivia is right in the centre of South America. It is three and a half times the size of the UK with the same population as London. The people are spread out across lowlands with jungle, highland valleys and even higher land called the *altiplano* where La Paz, the capital city, is located. This is the highest capital city in the world.

I was working on a project in a small village 35km from the city of Cochabamba, called Aranjuez. Effectively we were in the middle of nowhere. In the centre of the village was a square that always seemed empty, apart from a big tree in the centre of it. The houses were made of mud brick; cows and sheep wandered along the dusty streets. There were about three cars in the whole village and one shop that could not really supply our team of eleven's shopping requirements. So we did what the locals do and bought two rattling bikes. These were great fun. If we were not on the building site rota on a particular day, we could cycle off to the nearest town to buy food.

Building was good. We were helping the local evangelical church to construct their new meeting place. We did some bricklaying and got used to the scaffolding that bends beneath your weight, and worked on the floor. It was physically demanding. There was no cement mixer so the majority of the time was spent shovelling rubble and sand and wheeling it to a place to mix the cement. In the hot sunshine of the Cochabamba valley we not only discovered muscles we never knew we had, but we also got pretty exhausted. Our Bolivian co-workers could do twice as much work as us in a day but they were patient with us. They also could not believe that the girls were actually getting stuck into the work at all!

Aranjuez is not exactly one of the tourist highlights of Bolivia, so for many of the locals we were the first gringos (foreigners) that they had seen. As a result we really stood out in the area. I remember shopping one day and chatting to the owner of a stall whom I had never met before. He knew, though, that I was part of the group of young people who had come to do some building work. Having the bikes meant we could greet everyone as we passed on our way to the nearest town and, after initial stares, we would receive greetings back. Even people who did not speak Spanish, but only the Indian language of Quechua, would chat to us. If we bothered to try out some of the basic words we had learned, we were suddenly some fantastic source of entertainment.

We were living in two mud-brick rooms with mattresses on the floor. We had a kitchen with four gas rings and a plank balanced on some bricks to store food, and that was about it. We did not have a fridge or running water so we had to buy food every day. We did not know each other before we went to Bolivia but in the confined living conditions we got to know each other pretty quickly.

It also makes you find out lots about yourself. You tend to be so used to how you live and the way you do things that it is often not until you find yourself with a bunch of strangers that you realise things about yourself, like maybe you are not all that considerate after all. It is a real lesson in patience and a learning experience in how to love other people. My team most definitely became my family for six weeks.

I am not too sure what it is about Bolivians and food. As far as I can work out they seem to spend the entire time eating. Certainly food became a crucial thing that created much concern and joy throughout my time in Latin America. As a vegetarian I was the focus of vast amounts of worry to my Bolivian friends. They were not too sure how I managed to stay alive, and more specifically, how I had managed to grow so tall. This was no great achievement really as Bolivians are not a tall people. I was frequently confronted with a bit of a dilemma when our team was faced with evenings out with local families. Quite often it was just easier not to tell anyone and to hope that a dog would be roaming underneath the table at a vital moment. Alternatively I would sit myself next to Rob 'two puddings' who would generally be more than happy to help me out. These were never the ideal solutions. Bolivians are fond of extensive, unidentifiable soups where you usually come across a huge bone with meat hanging off it or, if you are really lucky, a chicken's foot. It is very rude to refuse this. At least if I had warned the family and had suggested the alternative of a fried egg, I would be able to have a little more than dry rice, potatoes and a bit of *picante*, a spicy tomato and chilli sauce. Cooking for ourselves was definitely my preferred option and even better were the times when someone's mum had posted out a bar of Dairy Milk chocolate.

We were all continually struck by the immense generosity of the people we met. I suppose that is why eating at the local houses could sometimes be a bit of a challenge as our portions were nothing less than mountainous.

All our water was collected from a well just outside our kitchen. Before we had arrived the people had dug two toilets and made two showers for us. These had two big oil drums above them that we had to fill with water from the well. On one of our first days there a few of the women from the church saw a couple of us washing our clothes in a big plastic tub outside our kitchen on the dusty floor. This upset them so much that they were determined to rig up a sink for us, making a tap that took water from the shower. Buying a sink was not a simple matter. While the ones we looked at seemed good enough, our local friends were not convinced by the quality. The situation was resolved when Constantino, a church member, insisted on lending us his sink that usually serves his family of eight, for the duration of the stay. This meant they went without.

Even on our last day we were amazed by their generosity. We had arranged to leave Aranjuez at ten in the morning. The night before we had a lengthy and tearful goodbye service so got up early to finish our packing. At seven I had just put the kettle on. The water must be boiled for twenty minutes so I soon learned to predict when we would want a cup of coffee. I was walking out of the kitchen in my pyjamas when I saw Maria, the Quechua-speaking wife of an elder of the church. Like us she had stayed at the church until after midnight for our emotional goodbyes but clearly she had been up much earlier than the rest of us as she was carrying a bowl of *picante* and a saucepan with a lid on. I was not too sure what was going on and in my best Spanish tried to make a joke about it being a bit early in the morning to be eating *picante*. It was a good job Maria could not understand me as it turned out that she had made us breakfast. In the pan were two types of boiled potatoes and boiled eggs. Not exactly a bowl of Frosties and a cup of tea but a great example of how much complete and genuine love these people showed us. A little later someone else arrived with a huge bowl of jelly.

We were given a lot of responsibility during church services, which was a real lesson in improvisation. The church met in a small mudbrick room which doubled as our dining room. The building we were working on would result in what is now a huge real brick church which is five times bigger than their previous meeting place. Although the congregation is growing, it seemed as if the project was too big and the new church larger than they needed. However that was just our European viewpoint and I was certainly challenged by the faith of these people who are poor in many ways yet who believe that their church will be filled and soon. The congregation had a vision for a great big church and so they set to work to build it even though they had no foreseeable prospect of finding enough money to complete it. What building would begin here without a clear indication that the money would be available to finish it?

At times it was a little frustrating for us with our Western ideas on how things should be done. We had a set amount of money and wanted to discuss what would be the most effective way of spending it on the church. We received few definite answers and bought materials little by little, unsure as to whether we would be able to complete the floor or the roof. This uncertainty annoyed us a bit. Don Nicholas, an elder in the church, seemed unconcerned when we asked him how he thought we should spend the money we had left, telling us that God knew where the rest would come from. Perhaps it is a bit socially unacceptable to respond with dismissive remarks like that here, I am not sure, but of course he was right. We were able to do all we had hoped to do and did not have any problems with the amount of money available. That kind of peaceful confidence that God had his hand on the work we were doing, was something we took time to acquire.

This vagueness extended to the church services which took place four times a week. As we were living right by the church it was no trouble for us to get there on time. It was working out what time they were meant to start that was the problem. We were told the Sunday morning meeting was from nine until eleven but having arrived on time we realised we were the only people there. It took us a while to get used to this different concept of time. Invariably nothing happened when it was arranged and locals quietly drifted in and out when they saw fit. As a general rule we would ask whether it was Bolivian or Christian time. There was roughly a half-hour difference between the two.

This came home to us with the Saturday night youth service. We were panicking a bit as we had two hours to fill but as our time in Aranjuez went on, we realised there was no need to prepare a service that long, as no one would arrive on time. It was more tricky when we were asked to do something in a service just as it was about to start! After being caught out a few times we practised some songs and drama sketches that we could do should we be asked. 'With Christ in the Family' was our most popular song as we could sing it in English, Spanish and Quechua but by the end of the six weeks we were thoroughly tired of it.

Two things came clear to me when I returned from Bolivia. I have to go back and I need to learn more Spanish for when I return. When I arrived at Heathrow stacks of other things hit me: carpet, flushing toilets, real chocolate. One of the first things I did when I got back home was to go to the local supermarket to buy a new toothbrush. I was completely overwhelmed by the bright lights and sheer amount of choice that was in front of me. I just wanted it to be simple. It felt strange to be back in my own environment.

In Bolivia I arrived with a group of strangers, to a place I had never been before, where they speak a language I only have a basic grasp of, to do a type of work I have never tried before. There was only one thing I knew was constant. The God who wanted me to go spans all boundaries of continents and this God was the only familiar thing I had to rely upon. It is an amazing thing really. The challenge for me is to keep that continual dependence and trust in him the rest of the time.

Growing in leaps and bounds

Name:	Sarah Bird
Organisation:	Interserve and Oasis India
Destination:	Bombay, India
Mission:	helping out in youth and children's work at school and in a church; taking English conversation classes in a tailoring company

After finishing my A levels in Biology, Art and Geography at Sixth Form college in June 1997 I went to Bombay, India for six months. I was working for Interserve's On Track programme and was seconded to Oasis India. In October I flew out on my own and met up with a team of eight others, mainly from England. We were the Frontliners, which is a short-term programme set up for school leavers.

While I was in Bombay I was mainly involved in the Valley of Praise church helping with the youth group and Sunday schools. Also I got involved in the projects run by Oasis.

'Jacob's Well' is a tailoring company set up to employ women, old and young, from the slums around the city. The aim is to train them for the working world, giving them experience and a trade they can earn money from, and also feeding their spiritual life. They also export their goods abroad, mainly to the UK. Some of the girls there could speak English but not fluently so I spent a couple of mornings a week talking and reading books, usually the Bible, with them. It was so good to see a working project and to be involved with it as it strived to improve its resources, to make a fairer trade between the developed and less developed countries, to reach out to more people and to touch more hearts where they were broken.

The people who worked there were a testimony in themselves. I will never forget their prayers of thanksgiving and praise before they started work in the mornings, their happy chatter and constant smiles.

I also helped out at a Christian school with two other English girls. New Life Academy had a mixture of children from different backgrounds and religions. The teachers were mainly Christians from many different denominations. The children were adorable and were very bright at an early age, since their teachers expected quite a lot of them.

The classrooms were small and they packed in the little desks. All the kids loved wearing their uniforms and were very well spoken since English is their first language. A lot of the time they would correct my spellings which really pleased them!

I went to Bombay with no fears, as my confidence lay in what I was doing and in knowing that God was taking me down a new and exciting path. I admit I did have apprehensions about what I would be doing out there but my excitement far exceeded that. By the end of six months I realised that I had much more to learn and to understand. That was going to be harder than flying to another country to live for a while.

My time there was exciting and I can say confidently, now that I am at university, that it was definitely worth taking a year out. I felt ready for university and had more of an understanding of what God wants from my life, what I want to do and how it fits into God's plan for me.

My decision to take a year out followed my newly found desire to work with people who do not have the comforts and luxuries that we are so used to. I wanted to encourage them and work close to them and share in their daily lives. Also my desire was to share with them something that is very close to my heart, that is that others may know God's love which is greater than anything else anyone can know. I wanted people to see that knowing God's love is far better than having to spend your time trying to keep the spirits at bay.

In India there are constant little rituals to keep the gods happy and the evil spirits away. For instance if children are very pretty they are given little black dots on their faces to make them less attractive to the spirits. Chillies are hung everywhere and incense burnt. Bright altars are put in the shops for different gods. The rituals are many, the gods are many and life is simpler, more fulfilling and without constant fear when people realise that Jesus is the only true saviour. To know that there is only one God and Jesus is the way to know him and that the Holy Spirit is the true spirit to guide you in every way is the route to freedom. It is sad that to so many people our God is one of many and Jesus is just another good man or prophet.

There are so many people needing to be reached out there in a world of materialism, gods and rituals, who are hungry for peace and understanding but who are trying to find answers in unhelpful places. These are the people that Jesus longed to reach, to touch and to heal. I became convinced that God wants to send out people to be like his instruments and his hands to others. I wanted to be ready, to be willing and to learn how to be of use. I realised I had a lot to learn. I do not think you can ever stop learning or understanding more about God because he is far greater than our human minds can grasp.

I did not particularly choose Bombay and had little inspiration to live in a hot, smelly, busy and poverty-stricken city. Somehow, though, I knew that God had closed the doors I had wanted open, and opened the doors he wanted me to go through. So I had to trust and put all my concerns and anxieties on him. All the time I was in India this happened. I constantly did not understand things or what to do so I had to trust God. My relationship with God grew in leaps and bounds but I also messed up. However I am so pleased that my relationship with him is far deeper and closer than I ever realised it could be. There is a deeper peace than I have ever known before and a security that tells me that I can call on God whatever the situation.

Going to Bombay was an experience I will never forget. It was a challenge. I came closer to God and I met people who gave me a greater understanding of what he is like and what I am like. The people out there supported me in a way I never expected and the people I knew back home were a great encouragement to me. It was brilliant!

Here for a reason

Name:	Laura-Jane Carson
Organisation:	OMF
Destination:	Thailand, East Asia
Mission:	to get immersed in another culture and live and work alongside long-term OMFers

Why did God bring me to East Asia that summer? I can think of a number of reasons, but one main one stands out. I think he wanted to show me that if I give up my small plans for God's bigger plan, he will help me to understand how he works, wherever that is.

I had been planning to go to Cambodia. To help prepare for going I had read a book called 'Killing fields, Living fields' by Don Cormack and Philip Yancey (Monarch Publications, highly recommended) and by the time I had finished the book I felt my heart was burning for Cambodia. I wanted to go to a place where people wanted to hear about Jesus. I wanted to meet Khmer Christians who have lived through persecution. I wanted to meet students in schools and universities and talk about Christ. I wanted to experience a place where life would be simple. I like to plan ahead so I read the Lonely Planet guide, learnt a few Khmer phrases, wrote to missionaries who were arranging my schedule… and then on July 6th political chaos hit Cambodia. All my best-laid plans had to change. I had to decide whether to go to Thailand anyway, since I would have been flying through Bangkok to go to Cambodia, or to cancel the trip altogether and go at a later stage.

Some words of wisdom from the principal of my college helped. He suggested that sometimes God wants us somewhere totally different in order to guide us more clearly, so, why not go? The point about faith is that we trust God when we do not know what will happen next. After all, when I thought about it, how many people of faith in the Bible knew exactly where God was leading them? Hebrews chapter 11 gives some amazing examples and I especially like what it says about Abraham, who left his home not knowing where he was going, in response to God's promise about the land he would later receive as an inheritance. So I left with the prayer, 'Lord, you can put me wherever you want.'

Five weeks later in a little village in an area where there are few Christians, I sat praying.

Thailand is beautiful and colourful, people are generous and kind and friendly, and the food is deliciously tasty and varied. I always enjoyed walking in the street or through the market, taking in the mouth-watering smell of spiced chicken cooking at one of the seemingly endless food stalls. Equally memorable is the pungent 'smelly socks' aroma of the special durian fruit, the only Thai fruit that presents a mega challenge to a foreigner's palate, definitely a taste to be acquired. Everywhere you hear the phut-phut of mopeds, which everyone rides, the ladies side-saddle. If it is raining they simply ride along with their umbrellas up and the drivers transport all sorts of goods from the local market.

At night I loved to listen to the constant chatter of tree-insects and the revelry of party-happy frogs in puddles, ponds and swamps. Not so pleasant is the all too familiar high-pitched bzzzzt of yet another mosquito, which you try to swat quickly, showing no mercy. Cute, shy gecko lizards dart along the walls in the evenings. They were soon my friends because they liked eating my tormentors, the mosquitoes.

The hot sun keeps the people in the shade during the earlier part of the day and in the rainy season by mid to late afternoon the humidity has built up to an in-your-face saturation point. Eventually a torrential downpour sends people scurrying for shelter, usually to their own home, as the rain can last for a few hours at a time. After the storm the air is magically clear again. The people I was staying with run English classes and they happened as long as it did not rain. If it rains no one may turn up. That's just the way life is. I could not help wondering if anyone would ever get to school in my rainy home country of England if we followed the same system!

As I had hoped, I had the opportunity to visit students in schools and university. This was through contacts made by OMF, whom I had gone to Thailand with. I was privileged to meet radiant Christians who had heard about Jesus through a leprosy clinic and I was very well looked after. Yet one morning as I sat praying something was niggling at me.

'Lord, I know you brought me here, but I am still thinking about Cambodia. Thank you for all the things I've seen, all the people I've met, but I can't do very much here. I can't speak the language and I'd like to help more. Please do something to show me you have me here for a reason.'

Six hours later I got on a bus and was squeezed into a seat with two high school girls, dressed in their Islamic-style school uniforms, faces peeking out shyly. I always liked using public transport. Somehow you feel you are right with the ordinary people and I love to watch faces and fashions and to pray for God's kingdom to come among them. These girls were curious about my foreign face and clothes and were intrigued by the little book of photographs of my home country and family. I was surprised to find my Thai phrase book could be stretched in order to talk about all sorts of things and within twenty minutes I had two new friends. To my surprise they asked my hostess, with whom I was travelling, if I could come and stay overnight at their house. They were going home for a couple of days from boarding school and they wanted me to go with them. It was one of those moments when it was clear that God was answering prayer and I was glad to accept their invitation.

After another bus trip, a long walk in the sun and a motorbike journey criss-crossing between country roads and tracks along the edge of rice fields, we arrived at their home, a typical house on stilts. Quickly I was immersed in a culture that was very welcoming and utterly different. There had been no time to ask questions or to prepare so I looked very much the stranger among them. I was given a sarong and instructions to wash and then taken on a tour.

The first stop was an ice stall. On hot days it is popular to buy a dish of ice, ground with an ancient machine that reminded me of some gadget out of my dad's garage, and serve it with coconut milk, syrup and fruit. Women and girls gathered there in the afternoon to talk and my young hostesses were proud to be able to introduce a foreign friend. I later found out that I might have been the first foreigner in this little village.

'Muslim?' asked the lady who was grinding the ice. I had my head covered in an effort to be more like the local ladies. I realised I did not even know how to say, 'I'm a Christian.' 'No,' I answered in Thai and could get no further.

'Buddhist?' they signalled, using the hands together kind of movement used by Thai Buddhist people. 'No…' I said, flicking madly through the phrase book which was being used more this afternoon than in all the five weeks I had been in the country. 'I…follow…Isa (Jesus).' I tentatively explained, wondering if it made any sense at all. Clearly it was understood. Like in a game of 'Chinese Whispers' the message was passed round the crowd of women.

'Christian…Isa!' I wondered what Christian meant to them or Jesus for that matter.

I wished I could say more but during the events of the two-day visit I learned to pray, 'Lord, please let them see you in my face. I can't say anything. You are the God who helped people hear the gospel in their own language at Pentecost. Please show them what you are like in some way through my being here.'

I was taken to meet neighbours, who served spicy papaya salad or some seasonal fruit as a treat, and was thoroughly inspected every time. Within only a few hours my friends had stories to tell about the funny way I washed, the funny way I ate, and the funny whiteness of my skin. At this point in the story-telling, which I started to anticipate, someone would inevitably try to pull up my sleeve to see just how white I was. They would squeeze my hand and arm, presumably to see if my flesh was different too. Their hands showed they were used to hard work, tapping rubber from the local plantation. My hands were those of a student used to pushing a pen and having clothes washed in a machine in a world far away. Yet the more I was in their company I saw that people are the same underneath the different clothes and culture. There are red apples and green apples but they are all apples. And Jesus loves the rubber workers just the same as he loves the student on the other side of the world. He died for us all.

At night before we slept the sound of the call to prayer from the mosque brought the day to a close. I started to read my Bible as usual at the end of the day. 'Read it out loud,' my hostess signalled. So with joy I read out a psalm and prayed that God would make his salvation known here in this family, in this village, among these people. I do not know what she thought, but I remembered being told that many people have wrong ideas about what a Christian is. They often think Christians are immoral, immodest, and idolatrous and they do not worship the true God. They hear in history that Christians went to war against Muslims and sadly they still think of Jesus mixed up with all these confused ideas about what the message of the gospel really is. Part of the job of the short-term worker is to *be* a Christian in the true sense of the word – a follower of Jesus among people who just do not know him. Actions speak louder than words, they say. Ideally we would love to be able to tell them the message but respect and love for God, humility, modesty, even accepting their hospitality graciously, can speak the truth to them, even without spoken language.

I cannot remember whether it was the rooster's crowing or the call to prayer which came first but it was early in the morning. No one needs a watch here. I wondered if it was more than a coincidence that my watch had stopped on the morning when I had been praying for God to do something. For a short while I could sense time just as the local people do with no need for hours and minutes. Five times a day the call to prayer is relayed to all parts of the village and the hunger in your stomach is another reasonable guide to time. The priority is just to do the next thing. If it is not finished today it can be done tomorrow.

We joined some women in the plantation as they collected sap from the trees. Then we had a break, indulging in some sweet, fragrant fruit picked on the spot from the trees by the house. I was taken to see the girls' favourite places, was thoroughly photographed using an old borrowed camera and was honoured to sample the best of their simple food cooked over a charcoal fire in an iron pot. They have an ingenious biodegradable waste disposal system. Any vegetable peelings are simply dropped through the slatted wooden kitchen floor and since the house is raised on stilts, the hens below enjoy what people cannot eat. The area under the house is also treated as storage space and there is a hammock to relax in or you can entertain guests in the shade on a raised platform.

I felt so honoured to be a guest in a home where people did not know anything about me. I could imagine how important it must be for Asian visitors to the West to be invited into a family home. No wonder the Bible encourages hospitality!

I also think it is important, when you go to another country, to go with an open heart to people and to God. I was brought back to the bus by motorbike and then accompanied on the bus all the way back to the Christian home where I had been staying. Not two but four drenched girls arrived home with me through torrential rain and were welcomed with towels, hot fruit tea and cookies. These girls went to great lengths for me. I am sure God will use our contact for his purposes.

Incidentally I did get to visit Cambodia for a short time before I went home and I was not disappointed. Out of the whole experience I learnt that when I am in God's hands it is easier to trust him to put me where he knows is best for me rather than to worry and to try wriggling into what I think is best – a pointless waste of energy really! I like Hudson Taylor's words: 'Be God's man, in God's place, doing God's work, in God's way.'

Ask God where he wants to put you. Be willing to go. Then be God's person there and whatever he gives you to do, do it, even eat the durian fruit that is served to you, smile and say thank you. He will show you how, if you ask him, and you can come home blessed in a way you could not have imagined.

Why did God bring me to East Asia that summer? What do you think?

Time to cross the border again

Name:	Michael Bousfield
Organisation:	OMF
Destination:	Malaysia, Thailand
Mission:	teaching and helping in a boarding school, teaching English in Bangkok

My year out working in another country actually came when I had finished a university course in Belfast. After three years of studying physics I decided that I wanted to do something completely different, but I also wanted to do it for God as well. After talking to a friend who had been a missionary in Thailand and writing to various organisations, while at the same time praying about the situation, I got a one-year placement in Asia with OMF (International).

Most of my nine to ten months abroad was spent at Chefoo School in the Cameron Highlands of Malaysia.

Chefoo is a boarding school run by OMF for the children of missionaries who are working in Asia. The school grounds are very extensive with a playground, football pitch, tennis court, six classrooms, a computer room, library, dining room and accommodation for all the children and staff. Around thirty-five children attended when I was there, ranging from five to twelve years old. The children are taught at six different levels but because of the small numbers, they are divided into three classes, each incorporating two levels of teaching. There are four dormitories, two for older boys and girls and two for the younger ones. The school term lasts four months and then the children get a two-month holiday with their parents. In one year the children spend eight months at school and four months with their parents.

The Cameron Highlands are a mountainous area north of Kuala Lumpur. There is one main road that twists and winds its way into the highlands, stopping at over 6500 feet above sea level. The region is densely covered with thick jungle while along the main road tea plantations cover the sloping hills on either side. These tea hills along with the wild tropical flowers and plants provide spectacular views along the narrow road into the mountains. At the same time large monstrous trucks passing you on the other side of the road can provide equally spectacular scares. The bigger vehicle always has right of way in that part of the world!

Chefoo is around 5000 feet above sea level and is

surrounded by jungle. It is near two towns, Brinchang and Tanah Rata on the main road. The temperature is about 23 degrees all year, which is refreshingly cooler than the rest of Malaysia. This is why people from Malaysia and Singapore often go up to the Camerons for a break from the tropical heat. There are many hotels and restaurants for passing tourists.

Being so high up you soon notice the dampness of the air around you. Clothes can go mouldy in a matter of days so all Chefoo wardrobes are fitted with light bulbs which stay on all day to keep the air dryer. There are many different kinds of wild life. I saw many beautiful butterflies and giant moths, lizards, frogs, snakes and many insects I had never seen before.

With learning to adapt to these new surroundings I was thankful that English is widely used in Malaysia and that English is the first language used in the school. The fourteen members of staff working at the school came from places such as England, Scotland, Australia and Northern Ireland. There was also a woman from Singapore and one from Korea working there. Living with people from my own culture in a foreign country really helped me to settle in and I made some very good friends there. As OMF recruit their workers from many different countries to work in Asia, the children come from places such as Korea, Singapore, Britain, Hong Kong, America and Canada. With all these varied nationalities it was amazing to see children forming close friendships with other children in the same dorm, even though they had totally different cultural backgrounds.

At Chefoo the staff were split into teaching or dorm staff. However as I was a short-term worker there I helped out on both sides. Throughout the year I taught PE, computers and took a recorder group. I also helped the older class with a project on electricity, which I did enjoy.

Every staff member gets a day off a week as well as a few Sundays and a four-day break in each term. When it was the turn of the dorm parents of either the older or younger boys' dorm to have a break I looked after that dorm for the day.

Looking after the dorm meant getting the children up in the morning, making sure they were dressed and had read their Bible notes, sitting with them at meals throughout the day, making them sandwiches in the afternoon and getting them bathed before being put to bed at night. Other duties included playground supervision after school and at the weekend.

I really enjoyed the dorm work a lot more than the teaching side of things. However it was easy to get tired and stressed out, especially if I had a lot of teaching to do and look after a dorm on the same day. The younger boys' dorm had eight boys in it and I found they needed a lot more of my time individually than the older boys did. There were fourteen boys in the older dorm and looking after them for four or five consecutive days by myself was both a lot of fun and energy-draining at the same time!

After I had spent my first term at Chefoo I travelled up to Thailand at the end of December. I first stayed in a town called Lopburi for two weeks with a missionary from Northern Ireland. In Lopburi there is a learning centre for all new missionaries who are going to serve in Thailand. There is also a church planting team working in the area and new missionaries are expected to get involved in some of the outreach activities that happen, like sports or local church events. I had a week of Thai orientation at the centre and had the opportunity to meet local Thai students who had connections with the church planting team.

I then went to the Baptist Student Centre (BSC) in the centre of Bangkok. This is run by Baptist churches in America and uses teaching English as a way of getting to know local people. Thai Christians managed the centre and Thai people taught English as well as native English speakers. As I was the only non-American foreigner teaching at the centre, it took a while before my students could understand my accent. It is strange to think that there could now be Thai people in Bangkok speaking English with an Irish accent!

I taught there for a full term of seven weeks and had five classes a week, each lasting an hour and a half. These took place in the evening and my students were older school pupils or adults who already knew at least a little English.

It felt intimidating at first with about sixteen students in my class. The only teaching experience I had had before this was the little I had gained at Chefoo in the previous four months. The staff at BSC treated me as if I knew what I was doing but I didn't! I was given books to use as materials in my class but more effort and imagination was needed to use the time well and I found this difficult. I felt very unprepared and useless at times although the Thai people were always friendly and showed a lot of interest during class.

During my time in Bangkok I stayed in a Christian hostel that housed students attending a university nearby. The people here were also very friendly and some of the students spoke English very well. They were always willing to go out of their way to make me feel at home and this really helped me to get through my time in Bangkok. I think they felt sorry for me being young, on my own and in a foreign country.

Although the hostel and BSC were both located in central Bangkok it could still take up to two hours to get from one to the other on the bus. I probably spent more time on the buses than I did teaching!

While in Thailand I found I needed to use Thai words that I had learned during my orientation, as English is not widely spoken there. This was a pleasant change from Malaysia as I enjoyed trying to communicate with local people in their own language. It was a challenge to do this at times but in the end I would get there by using hand gestures, while the person I was talking to would be laughing at my attempts to get the right tones for the right sounds. The Thai use five different tones, giving each sound the possibility of five different meanings.

Once my seven weeks of teaching were finished I went back to Chefoo school to complete my second term there which finished in June.

Overall I was very glad that I took the year out in Asia. There were ups and downs, as anyone would expect, but this experience is something I will always treasure. I especially learnt how to rely on God for everything. During my stay at Chefoo there were times when I felt very stressed as I was finding some of the teaching difficult. Living with nearly fifty other people in an isolated environment also added to the pressures at times. But looking back I found that God needed to knock me down on occasions so he could rebuild me the way he wanted me to be.

I also found myself relying more on his protection and guidance, especially when I was travelling. As I was a short-term worker in Malaysia I could only stay there for two months at a time. This meant I had to travel a lot out of the country so I could get another two-month Malaysian stamp on my passport as I came back into the country. I was always travelling on my own and at times I was not sure how I was going to get to my next destination. For example, the train journey between Bangkok and the Cameron Highlands took twenty-seven hours. This included a quick change of trains and then a two-hour taxi drive up to the school. Seats on a bus or coach could not be booked more than one or two days in advance. Looking back on my journeys I can see where God was looking out for me.

Another thing I was able to do was to meet missionaries actually where they were working. I also met them when they were visiting their children at Chefoo or when they came to the Camerons for a break. I was able to get involved a little with the church-planting ministry in Lopburi as well as English teaching in Bangkok.

I had never fully realised what it was like for a missionary before I went to Asia. I found it hard to imagine what it would be like as a parent to say goodbye to your five- or six-year-old child as they leave for four months to go to school. I think this would be harder on the parents than the children. It is a real necessity and responsibility to look after the educational, emotional, physical and spiritual needs of missionary children. I am very thankful to God and feel very privileged to have been able to serve him in this area of mission. I do not know what I will do in the future but I am not worried. I know that God has a plan for me, as he does for everyone.

Organisations and Contacts

Abernethy Trust
Lorimer Gray, Abernethy Trust, Nethy Bridge,
Inverness-shire. PH25 3ED. Tel: 01479 8211279

Working at an outdoor activities centre usually on
the house/catering team. Average age 20.

- Full range of catering and/or cleaning duties
- Part of team aiming to share good news of
  Jesus with guests eg: helping with BBQs, sing-
  alongs, games evenings, Bible discussions,
  drama
  group, music band etc.
- Suit committed Christians who want to serve
  God in this kind of outreach
- Opportunity to join in outdoor activities
- Accommodation, meals and salary provided
- Twelve-month position initially

Crosslinks
Margaret Harding, Crosslinks 251 Lewisham Way,
London SE4 1XF. Tel: 0181 691 6111

SMILE programme, stands for Student Mission
Involvement Learning and Experience
  Gap year students work alongside an already
established mission partner using their skills in
their chosen interest fields eg: building, IT,

teaching. They help out generally and encourage others in the local church and share their faith.

Crosslinks also sends small teams to assist with children's clubs
Ireland, Spain, Kenya, Tanzania, China
Commitment varies, usually 2–6 months.

Interserve
Dave Taylor, Interserve, 325 Kennington Road, London SE11 4QH; Tel: 0171 735 8227; e-mail: ONTRACK@isewi.globalnet.co.uk

Interserve is an international, interdenominational fellowship who have a desire to live out their faith in word and action in another culture
Works in South and Central Asia, Middle East, North Africa.

Involved in evangelism, building up the local church, training church members and leaders, serving poor and marginalised people.

Ontrack is the short-term programme – a few weeks up to one year and has two aims:

• To encourage an interest in cross-cultural Christian service overseas;
• To provide an opportunity for Christians to experience living, working and sharing their faith in a cross-cultural environment.

The programme can place people in their gap year, for summer programmes, electives, new graduates, professionals and retired people.

Latin Link

Special Programmes, Latin Link, 325 Kennington Road, London SE11 4QE

Run two short-term mission programmes, for committed Christians, over 18, with an active church involvement.
   Stride Tel: 0171 207 5877;.
e-mail: stride.uk@latinlink.org
   Latin America
   Individual placements
   Six months to two years, starting each September
   Opportunities in school and TEFL teaching, children's work, agricultural work, church work, prison work and much much more.

STEP (Short Term Experience projects)
Tel: 0171 207 5880. e-mail step.uk@latinlink.org
   Latin America
   Live and work alongside Latin American Christians in a basic building project and church work
   Spring programme, 4 months, March–July
   Summer Programme 3–7 weeks, July–September

Life Ministry

Arnold Nzova, Information Manager, The Life Ministry, POBox 62500, Nairobi, Kenya.
e-mail: LFKENYA@MAF.ORG

OM (Global Action)

Gary Sloan, head of personnel, OM, The Quinta,
Weston Rhyn, Oswestry. SY10 7LT
Tel: 01691 773388. e-mail:info@uk.om.org

Global Action offers many opportunities for
training and service in many different countries.
   Choose from one of 3 tracks:

1. Action Evangelism Teams
2. Special Ministry Teams (Relief Ministries)
3. Vital Support Teams

18 +, commitment 1–2 years
Two intake dates, January, August

OMF International

Shirley Davy, OMF International, Station
Approach, Borough Green, Sevenoaks, Kent TN15
8BG
Tel: 01732 887299. e-mail: short@omf.org.uk;
web page www.omf.org.uk/short
   Work in East Asia to bring the gospel to those
who do not know Christ.
   Immerse yourself in another culture. Learn
more about the gospel and real life, more about
yourself and more about Christian service.
   Live and work with long-term OMFers and get
the inside track on what it takes to give your life
for others. Faith stretching. Can be tough! Make
your life count.
   Commitment, one month to two years.

18+, have a maturing relationship with Christ, be outgoing, flexible and adventurous.

Go as part of a team or have a 'custom-made' trip especially for you.

Openings for those with a wide range of skills eg: English teachers, child care, labourers, hospitality in mission home, student work, computer whizzes, admin/office staff, artists, hostel workers, school teachers.

Scripture Union
Phil Wason, International Relations Consultant, SU, 207–209, Queensway, Bletchley, Milton Keynes, MK2 2EB, Tel: 01908 856000, for enquiries for South Africa, Zimbabwe, Europe and Ukraine.

Gillian Taylor, Action Abroad Scheme, 13 Mead Way, Hildenborough, Tonbridge, Kent. TN11 9HA. Tel: 01732 833063, for enquiries for S. India.

Action Abroad offers volunteers the opportunity to get involved at Cornerstone House and the Scripture Union Camp Centre at Mahabalipuram, a beach side site, and at the Avalanche Adventure Centre at Nilgiris, in the mountains.

* Manual work and building projects
* Caring for children/families
* Outdoor adventure activities
* Camps, music, drama
* Schools missions

- 'Making Jesus Known' clubs in the villages
- learning from SU workers
- working as a team

For anyone 18–30, willing to discover more about themselves and mission.

Need to be flexible, adaptable, tolerant and ready to live rough.

Volunteers wanted for up to six months.

Gain valuable experiences into developing world cultures and get involved in overseas mission. Life-changing and challenging.

The Scripture Union Year Out Scheme
Claire Hornett, Scripture Union,.
207–209 Queensway, Bletchley, Milton Keynes,
MK2 2EB, Tel: 01908 856170

During the year you will get 'hands on' experience with experienced schools workers and evangelists:

  in urban *and* rural areas
- in large scale one-off events *and* small scale, long-term relationships
- in local areas *and* on national holidays or missions
- in one area *and* in short placements around the country

Soultime

Rachel Shorey, Soul Survivor, 7 Greycaine Road, Watford, Herts, WD2 4JP. Tel: 01923 447070

5-month course, aims to broaden young Christians in every way helping them to go on and live lives which bring glory to God.
* Intensive teaching programme
* Social concerns assignments
* Training in worship leading, public speaking, evangelism
* Close pastoral support
* Integration into church life and ministry of Soul Survivor, Watford
* Option to help run summer conferences based in Somerset (Spring course) or to fly to a developing nation to join in the missions work (Autumn course)

YFC

The Recruitment Secretary, PO Box 5254, Halesowen, West Midlands B63 3DG. Tel: 0121 550 805. e-mail: YFC@compuserve.com

All projects are geared to youth evangelism and discipleship.

Operation Gideon, radical discipleship training in youth work and evangelism, working in teams with churches and YFC centres. Minimum commitment, one year. Ages 17–28.

Various creative teams who use music, dance and drama to reach teenagers mainly in schools in UK and abroad. Some regional, others national. Minimum commitment, one year. Age 18–25.

Apprenticeship scheme providing a flexible training course in youth work where we work with each individual to design a programme which best suits their requirements. Minimum commitment, one year. Age 23+.

Street invaders. 3-week summer training in evangelism and social action, equipping young people to communicate their faith through friendship evangelism. July/August. UK and abroad. Age 15–25.